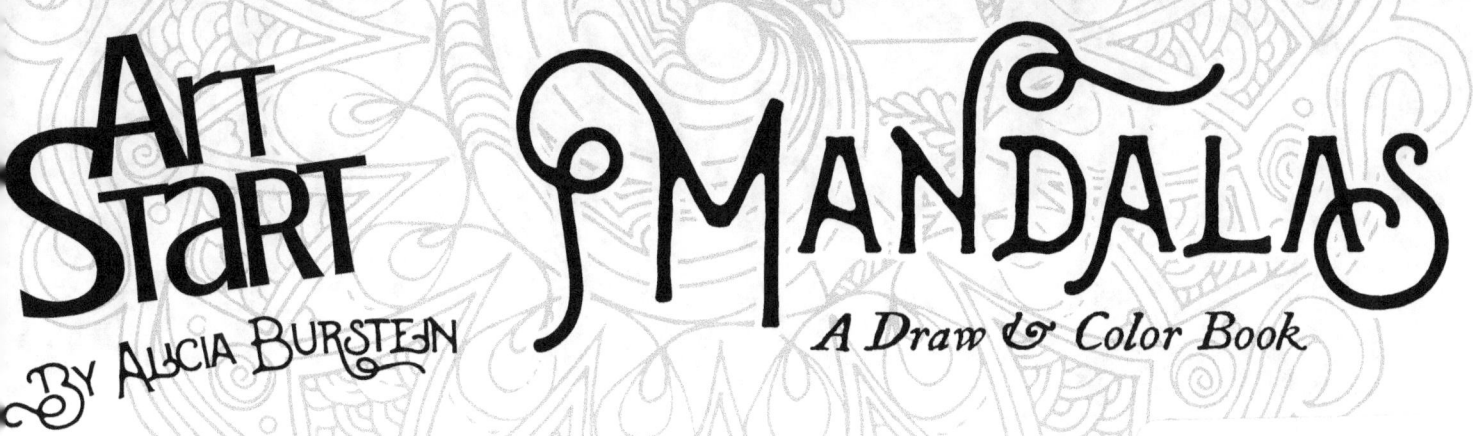

Art Start

By Alicia Burstein

Mandalas

A Draw & Color Book

I0473059

Welcome!

This Draw & Color Book is dedicated to the evocative and inspiring Mandala. Mandala, Sanskrit for 'circle', represents the universe, wholeness and balance.

In this workbook I have included a variety of ArtStart mandala exercises to get your creativity flowing. There are two levels of 'completeness' that you will find – mostly done and bare bones measured starters.

The mostly done mandalas are a great way to relax, flex your color theory and add in your own details. Don't be afraid to add in fills, extend the circles and create an art collaboration.

The grey starters are for you to create your own works of art. I found the part that discouraged me from the beautiful symmetry of mandalas was...well...the symmetry of mandalas! Mine never came out straight or equal and instead of relaxing they frustrated. Using the ArtStart guides will allow you to skip the ruler and jump forward to the ART!

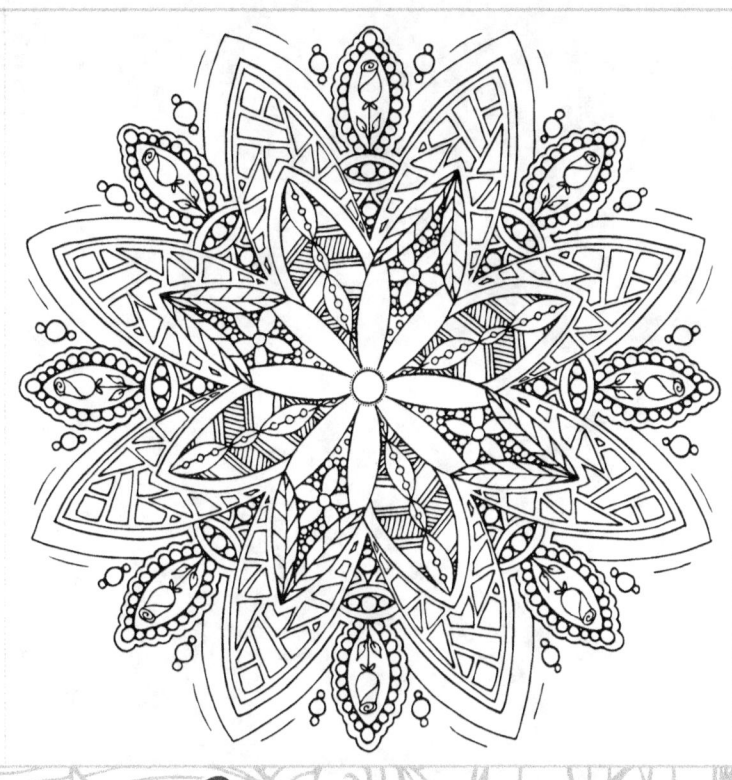

HAPPINESS IS RECEIVING A LOVE LETTER.

✂ Photocopy page onto card stock, then color, cut and fold. Cards are sized to fit in the envelope template.

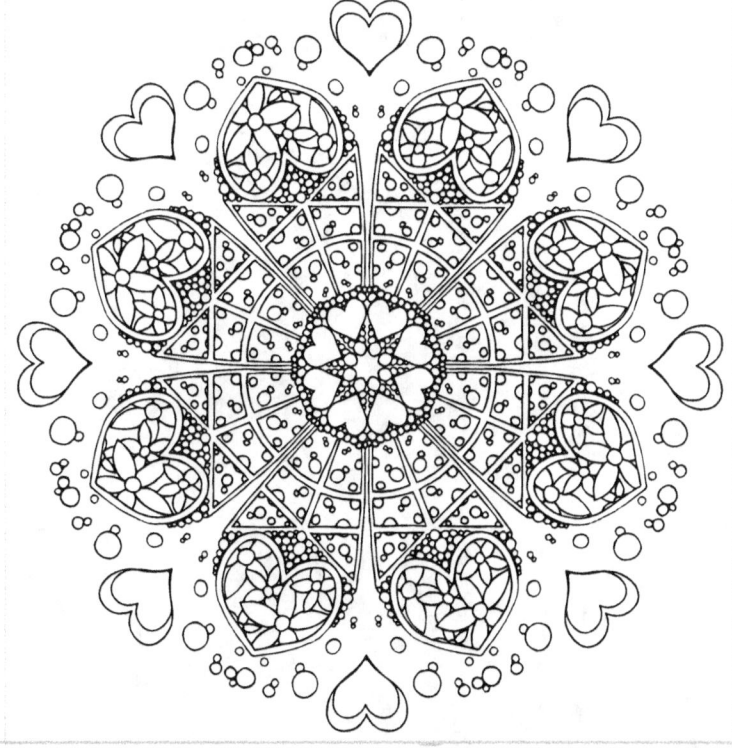

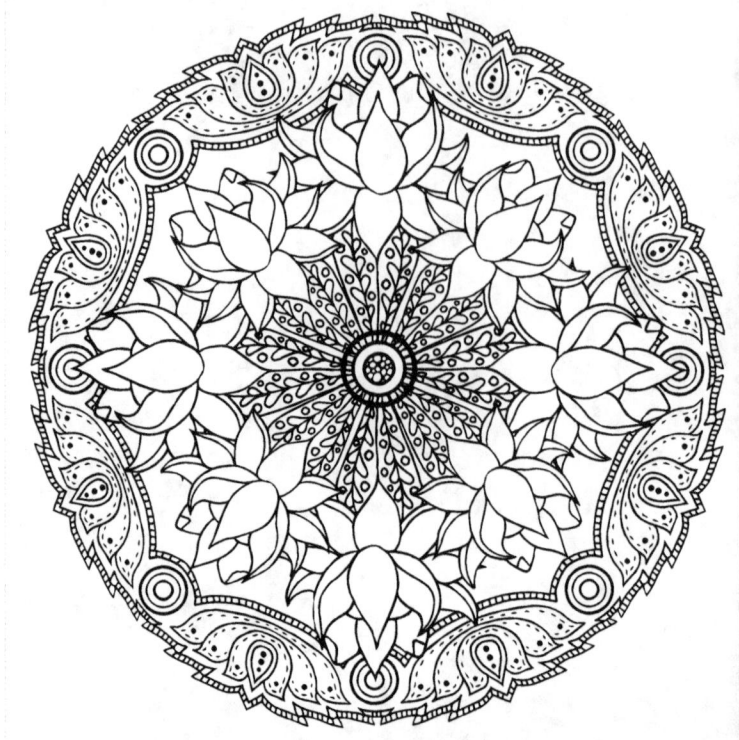

HAPPINESS IS RECEIVING A LOVE LETTER.

✂ Photocopy page onto card stock, then color, cut and fold. Cards are sized to fit in the envelope template.

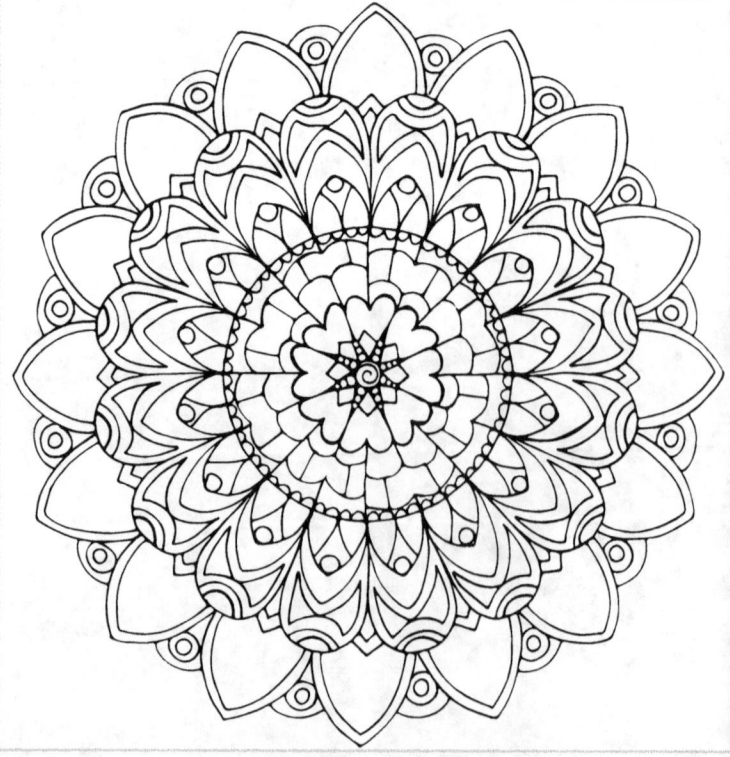

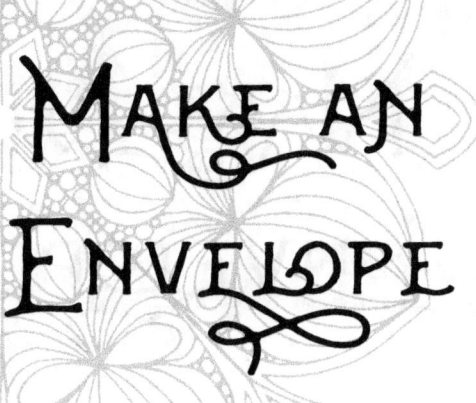

Make an Envelope

Use this template to make your own personal envelopes. Photocopy onto cardstock, color the designs and then cut out and assemble.

This envelope fits square cards 4inx4in.

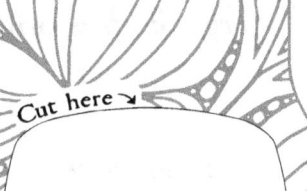

Cut here ↘

Fold on dotted lines ↘

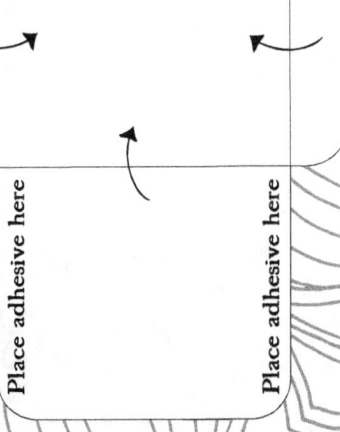

Place adhesive here

Place adhesive here

Inside of Card

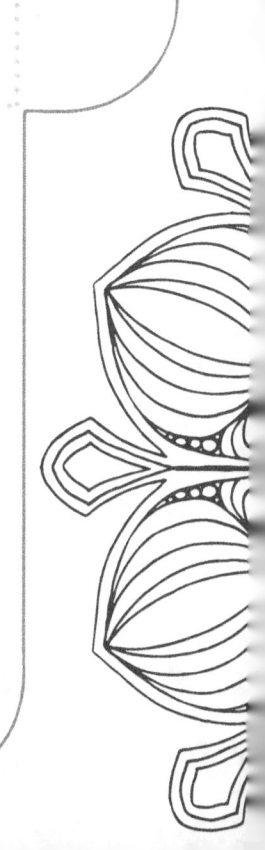

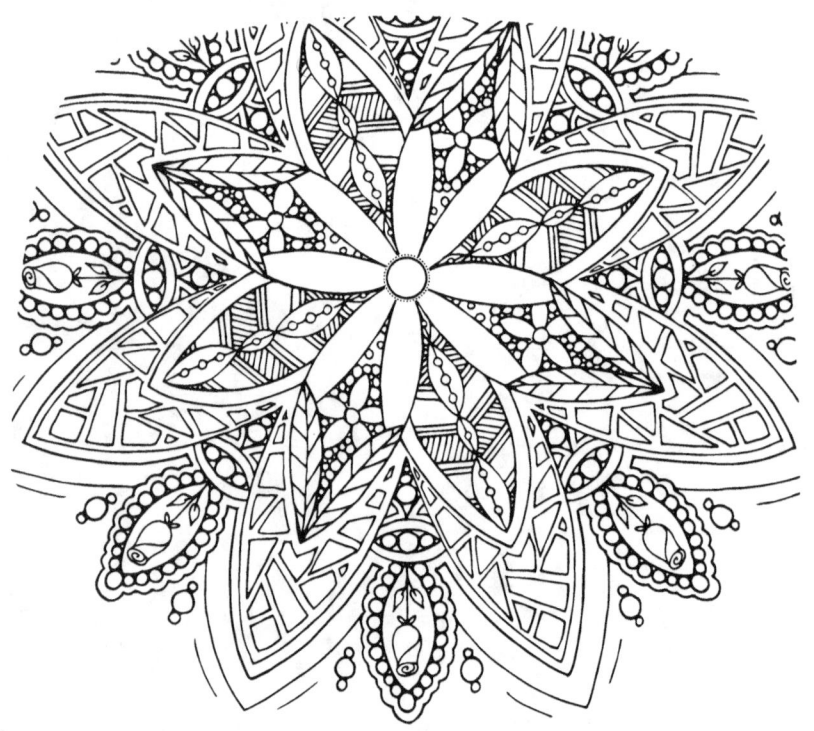

Make an Envelope

Photocopy this on the back of the previous page for a beautiful envelope design colored by you!

For even more personalization leave the front blank and draw your own designs.

You can also use this as a template and trace it onto some gorgeous pre-printed papers.

Everyone loves a note in the mail!

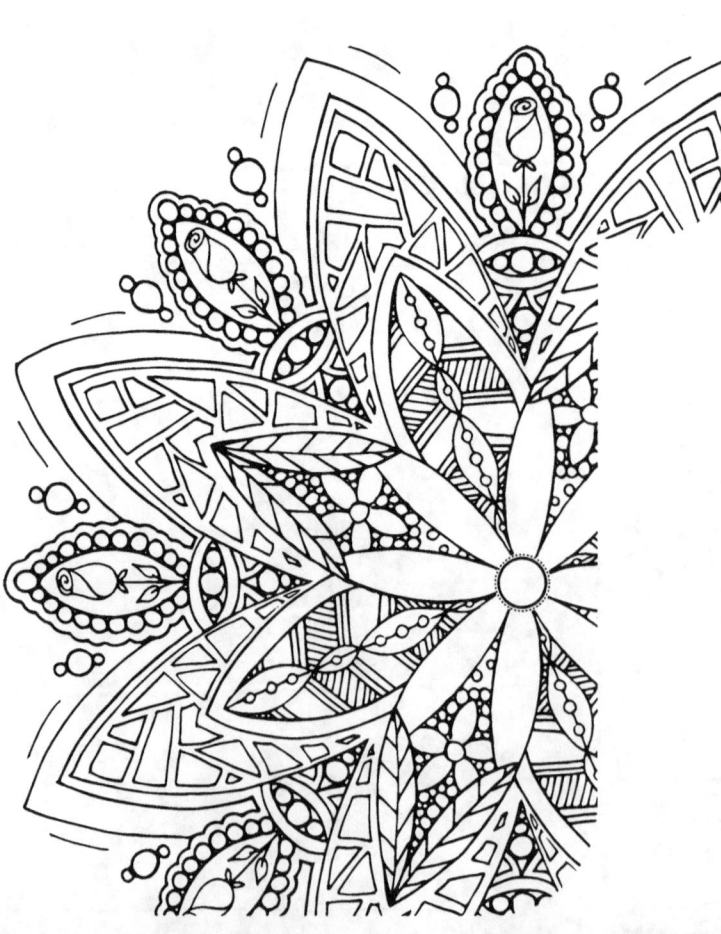

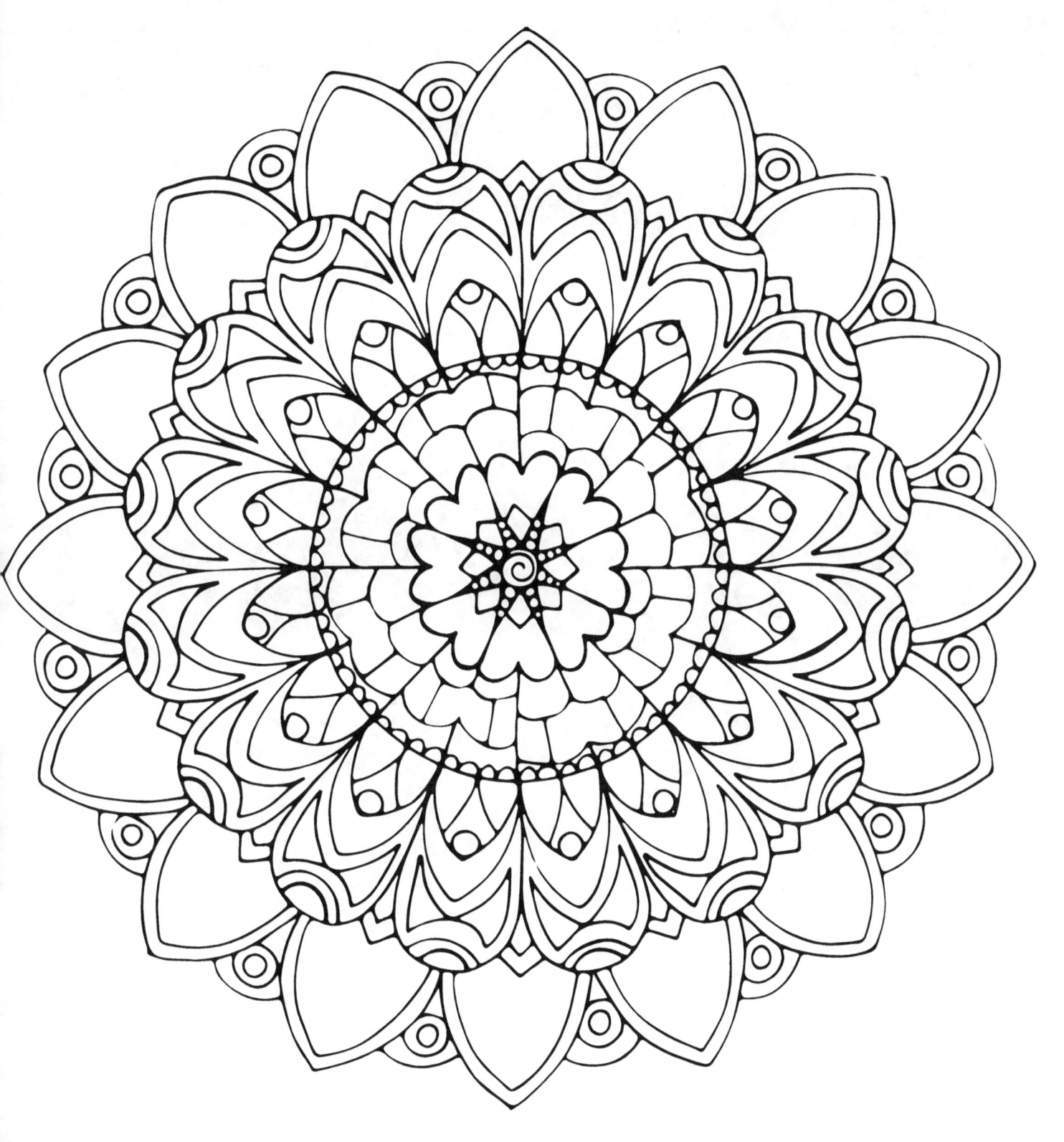

Nothing can dim the light that shines from within.

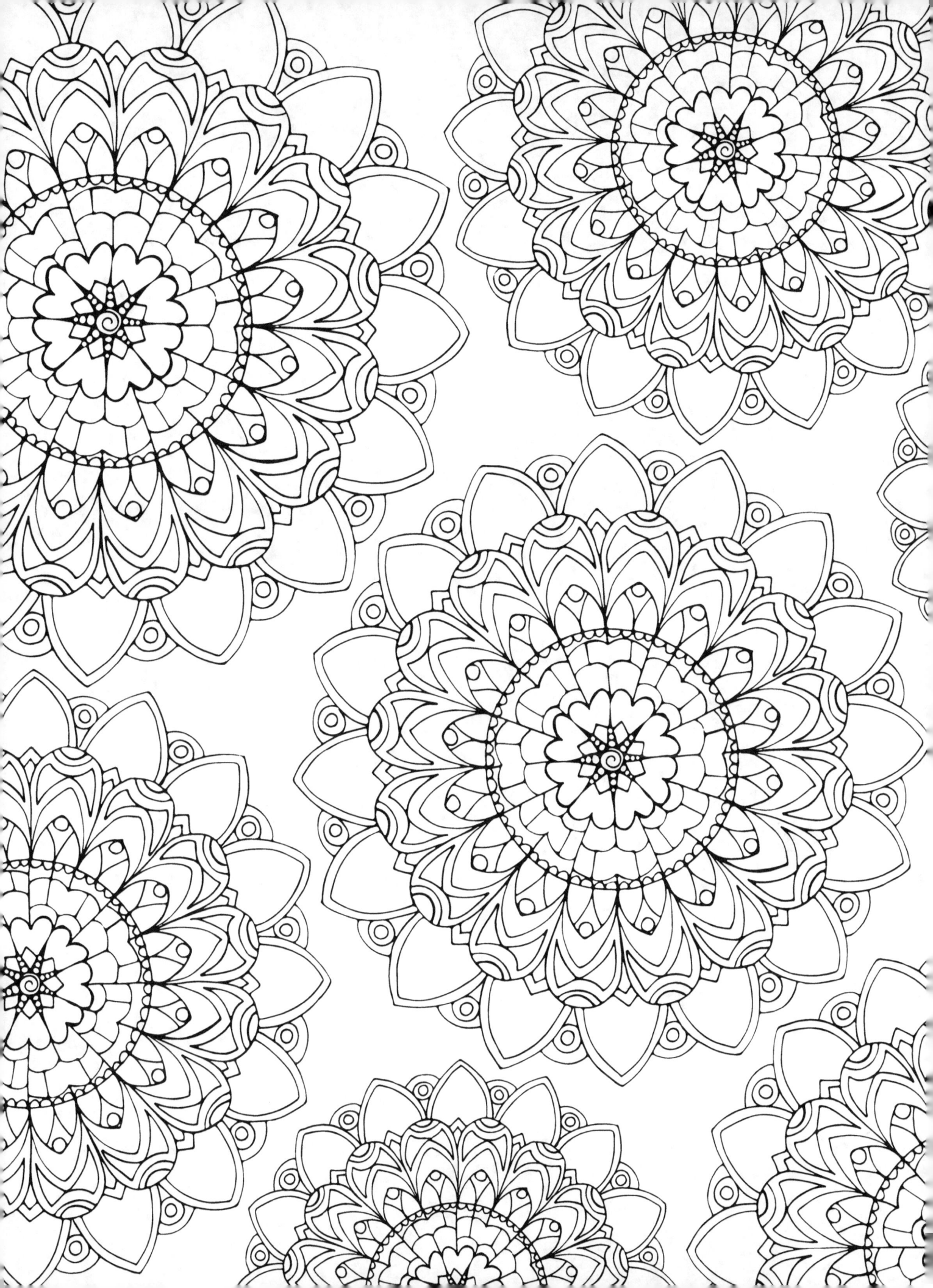

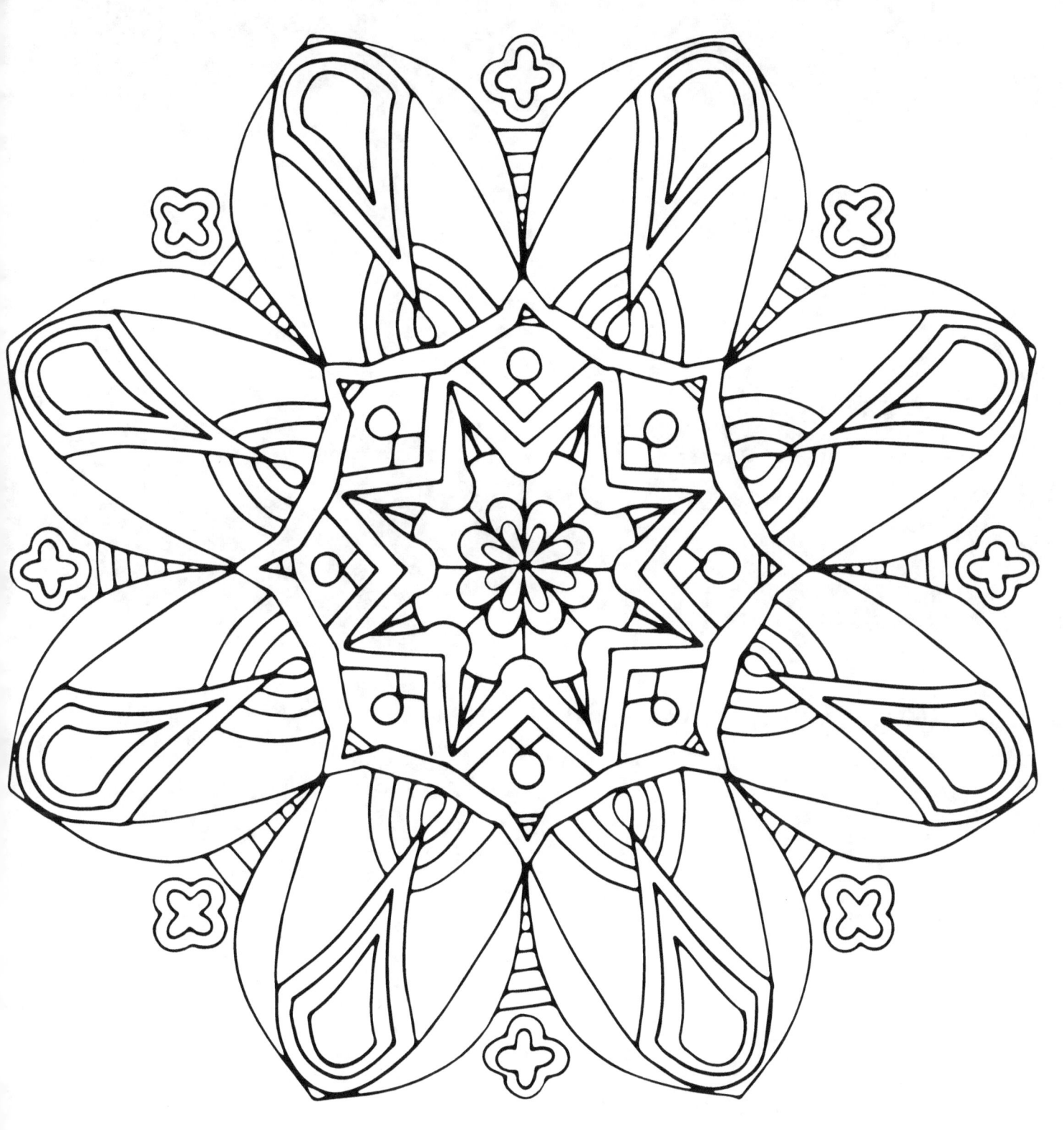

EVERYDAY DO SOMETHING THAT WILL INCH YOU CLOSER TO A BETTER TOMORROW.

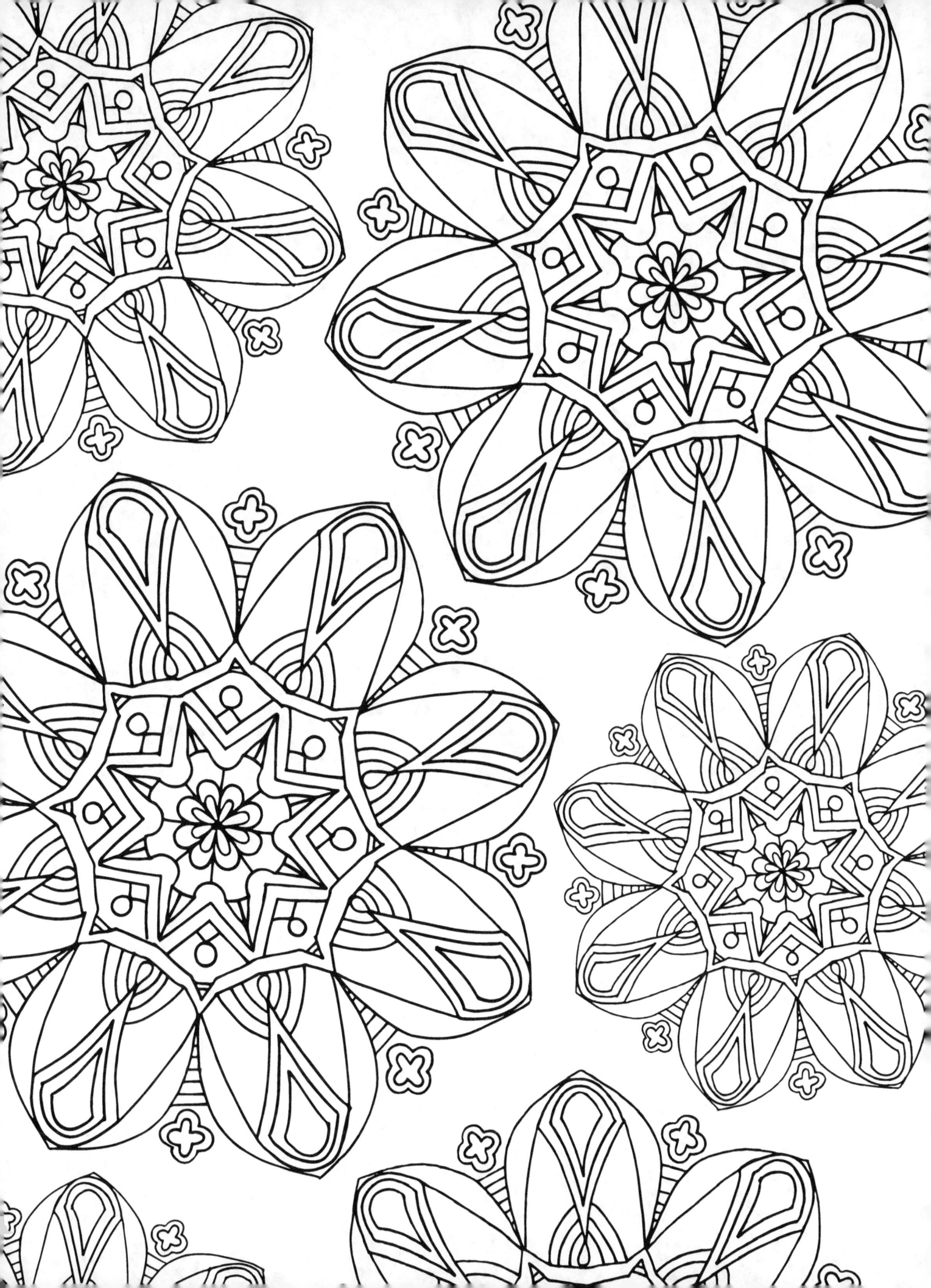

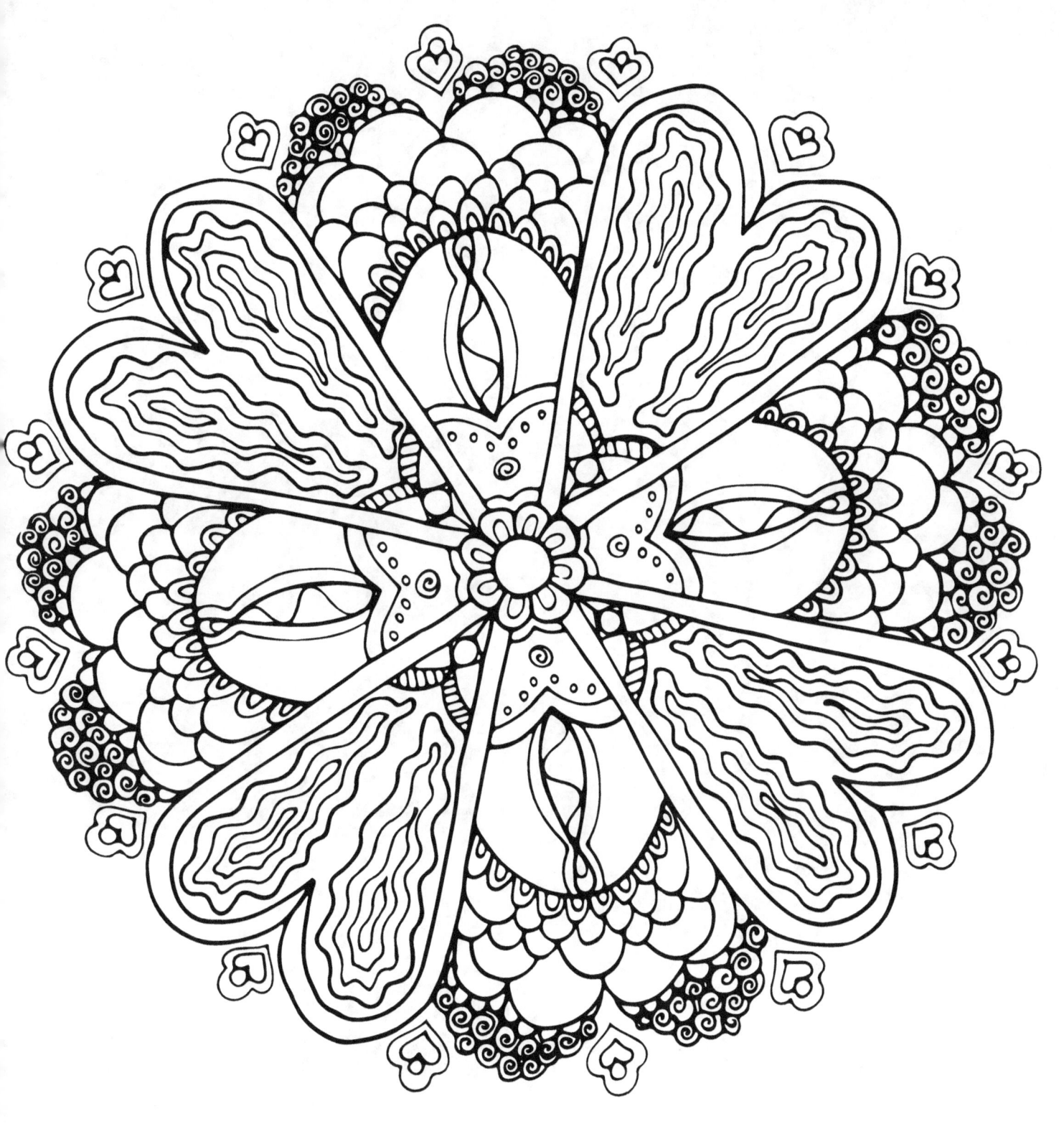

FRIENDS ARE THE FAMILY WE CHOOSE FOR OURSELVES.

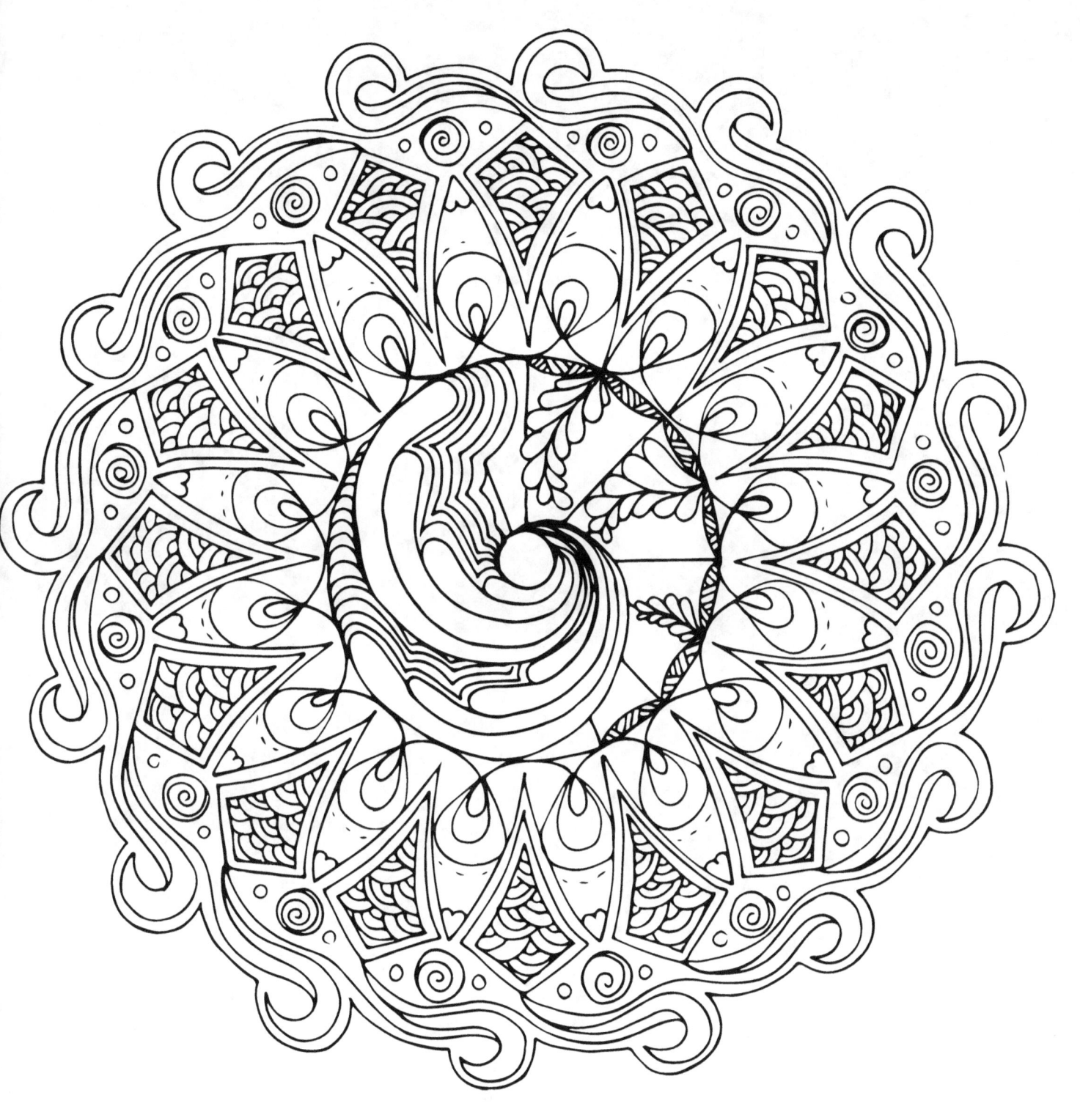

The Earth has music for those who choose to listen.

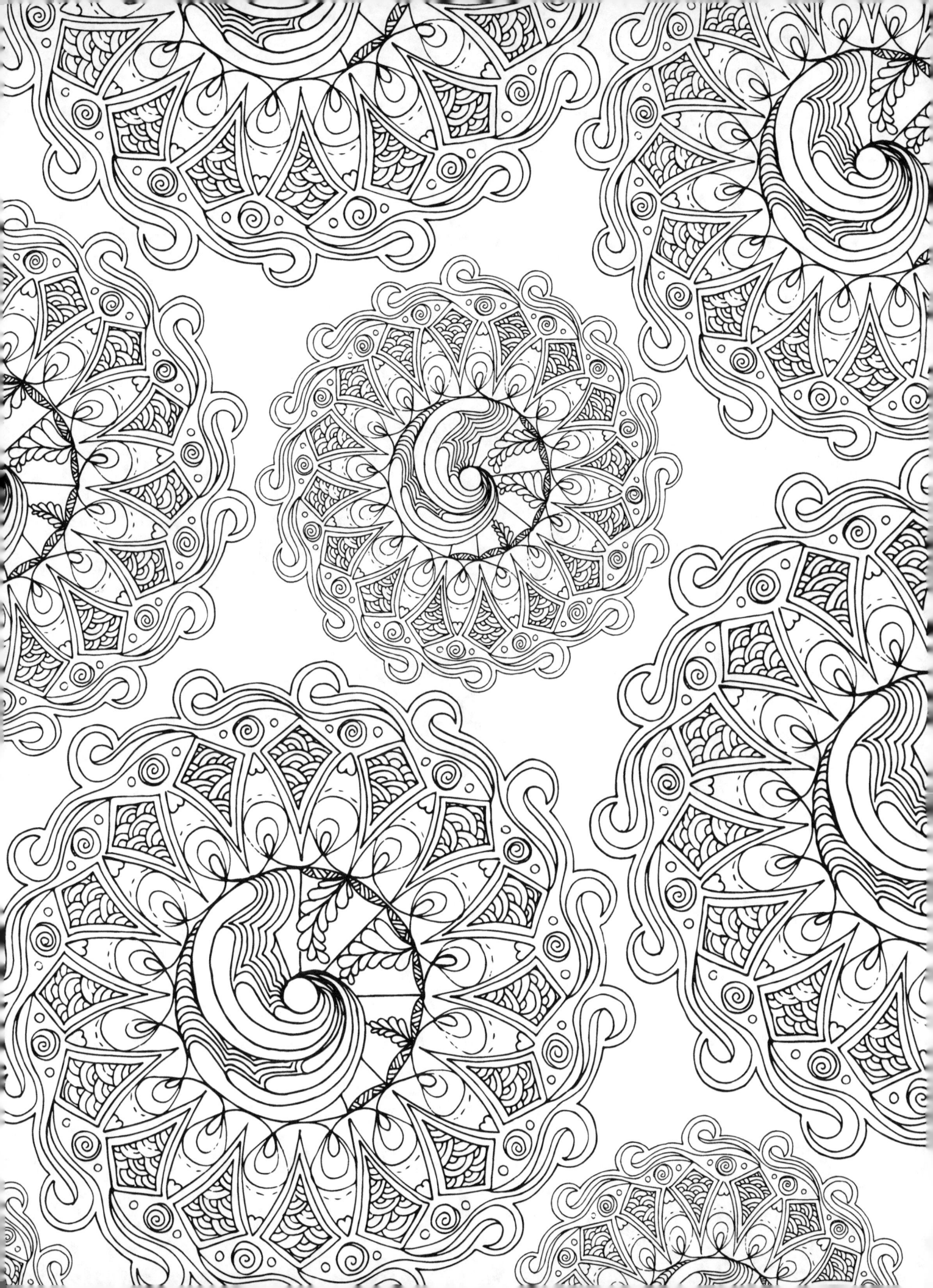

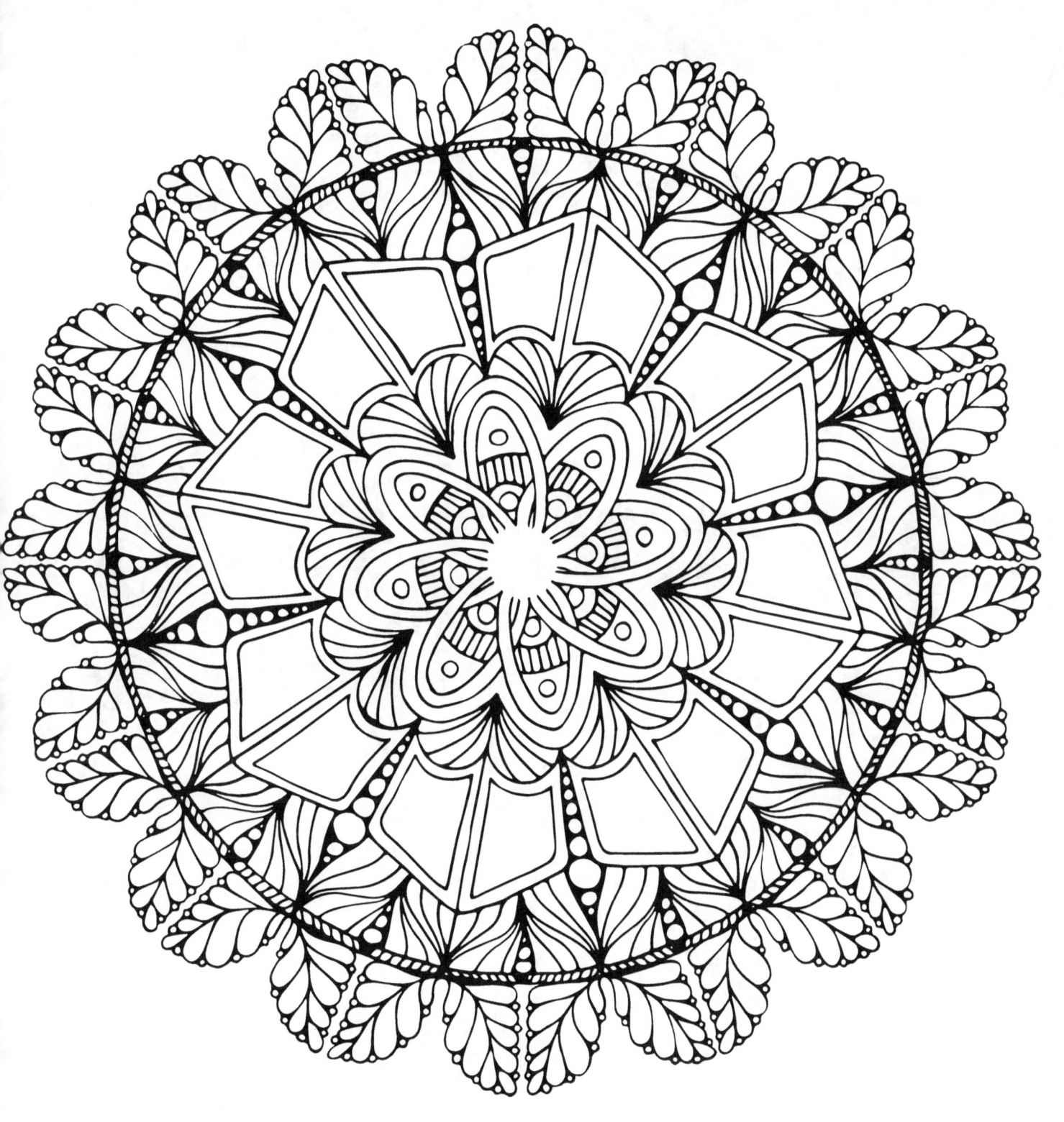

Let the beauty of what you love
be what you do.

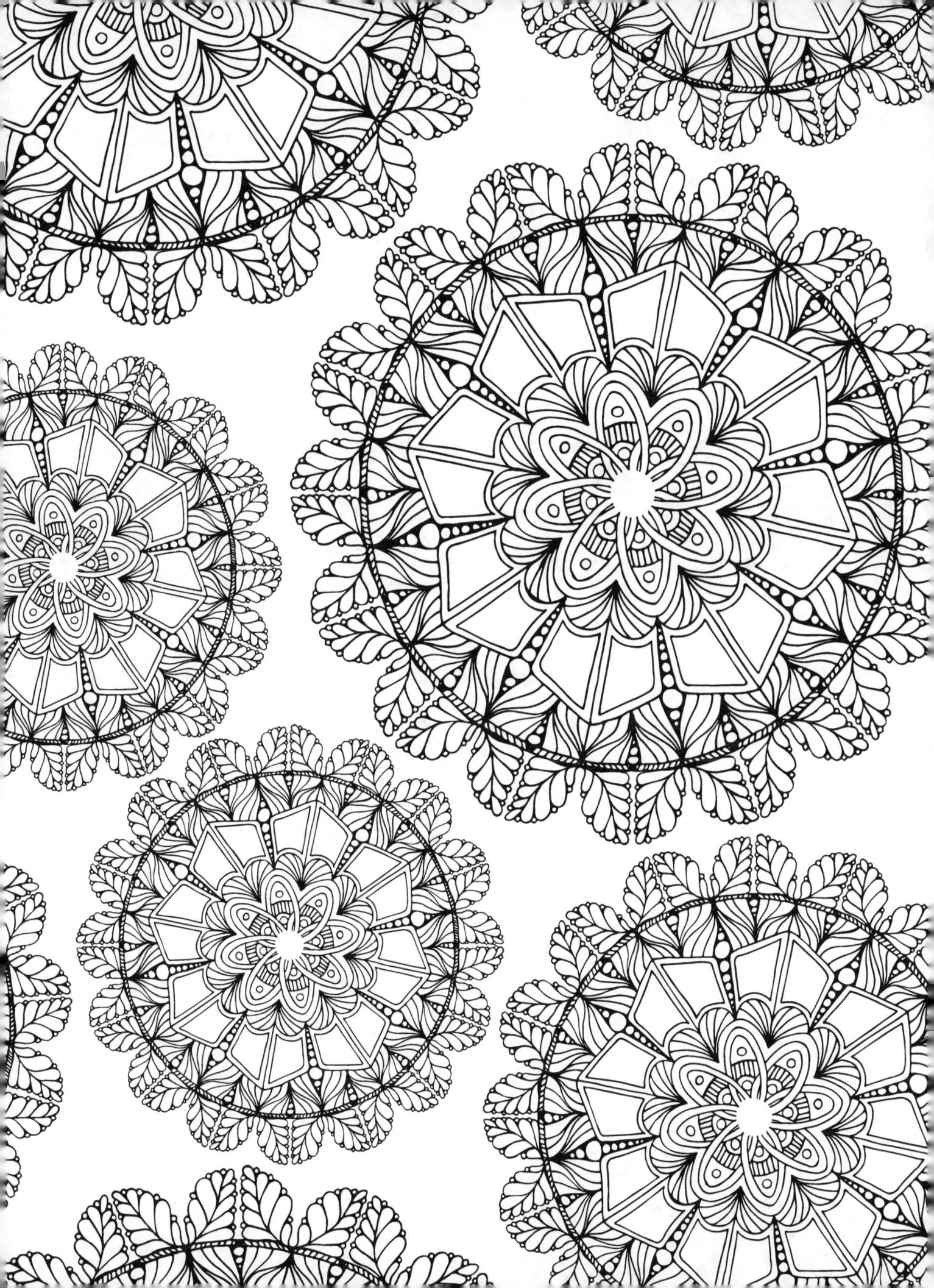

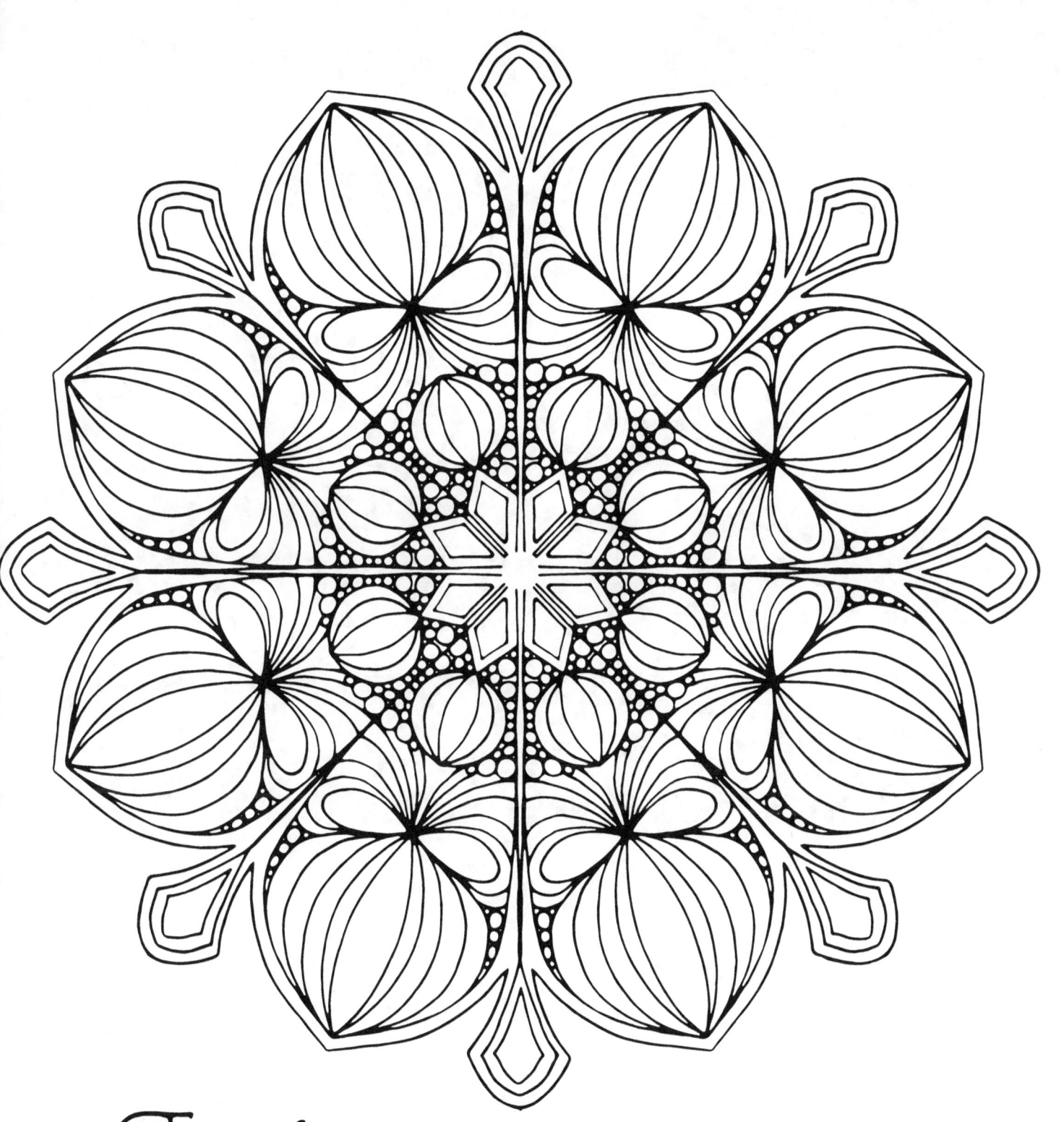

ENJOY THE LITTLE THINGS IN LIFE....
ONE DAY YOU'LL LOOK BACK AND REALIZE
THEY WERE THE BIG THINGS.

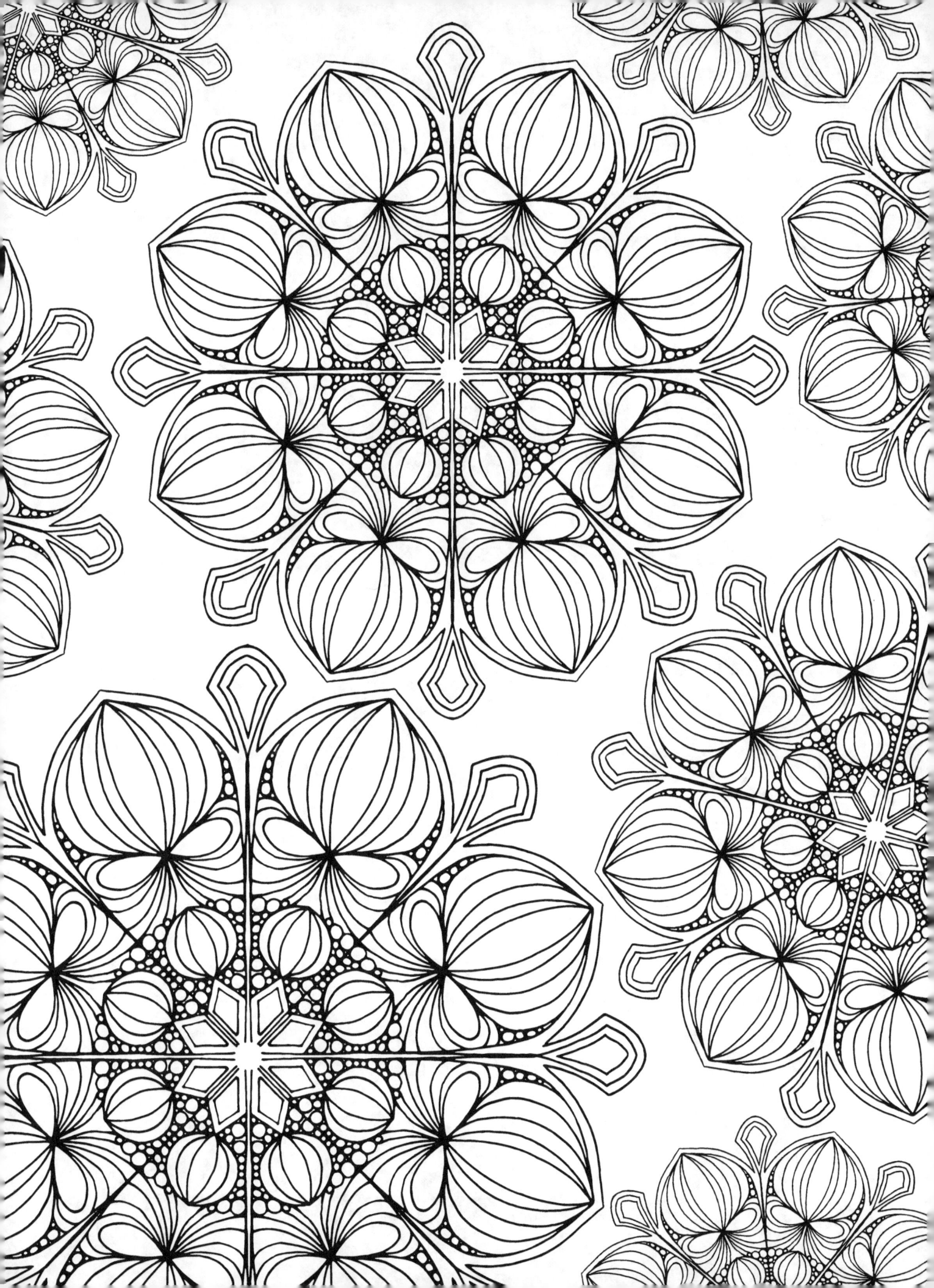

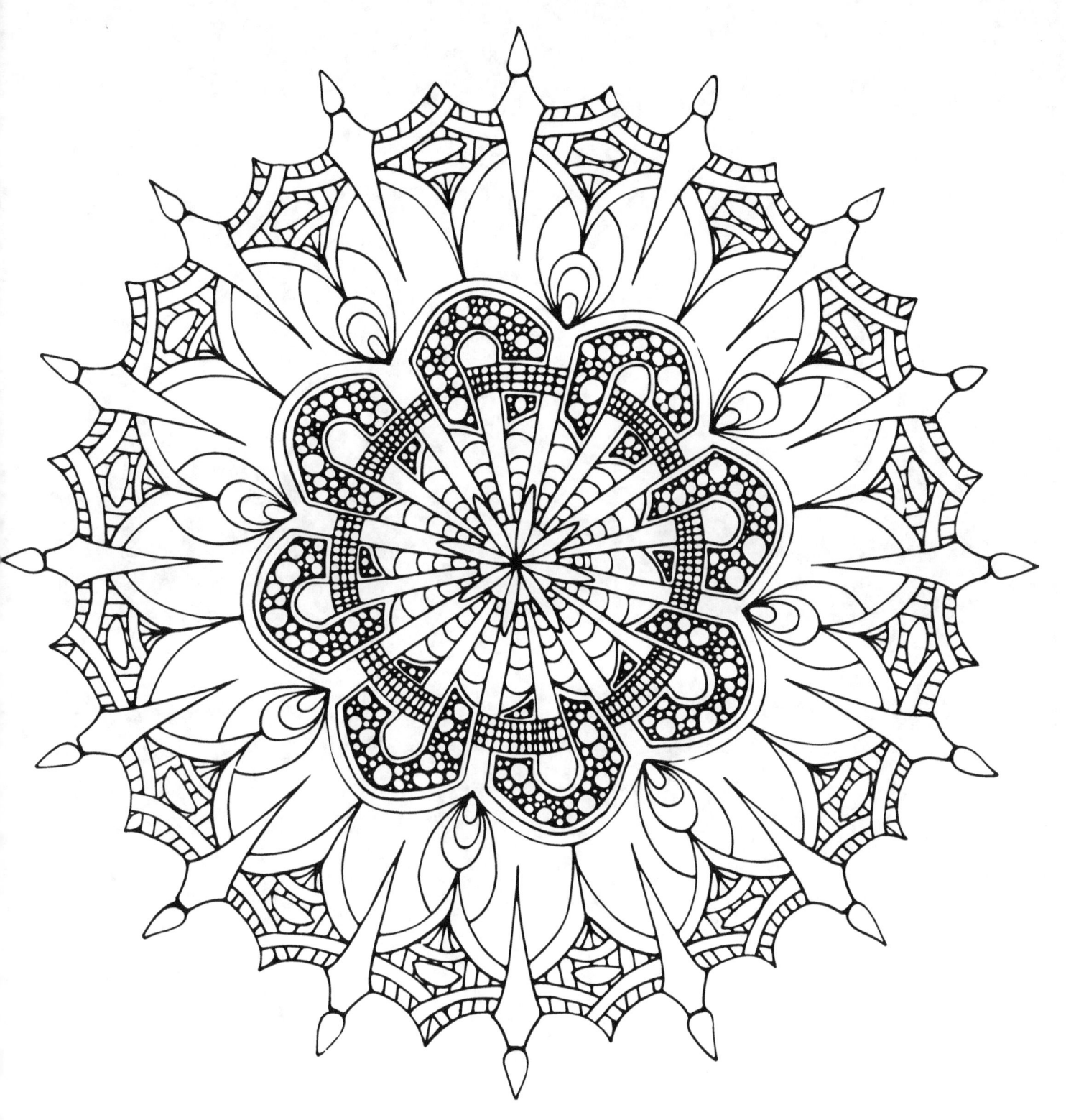

FORGET THE REASONS IT WON'T WORK AND
BELIEVE IN THE ONE REASON IT WILL.

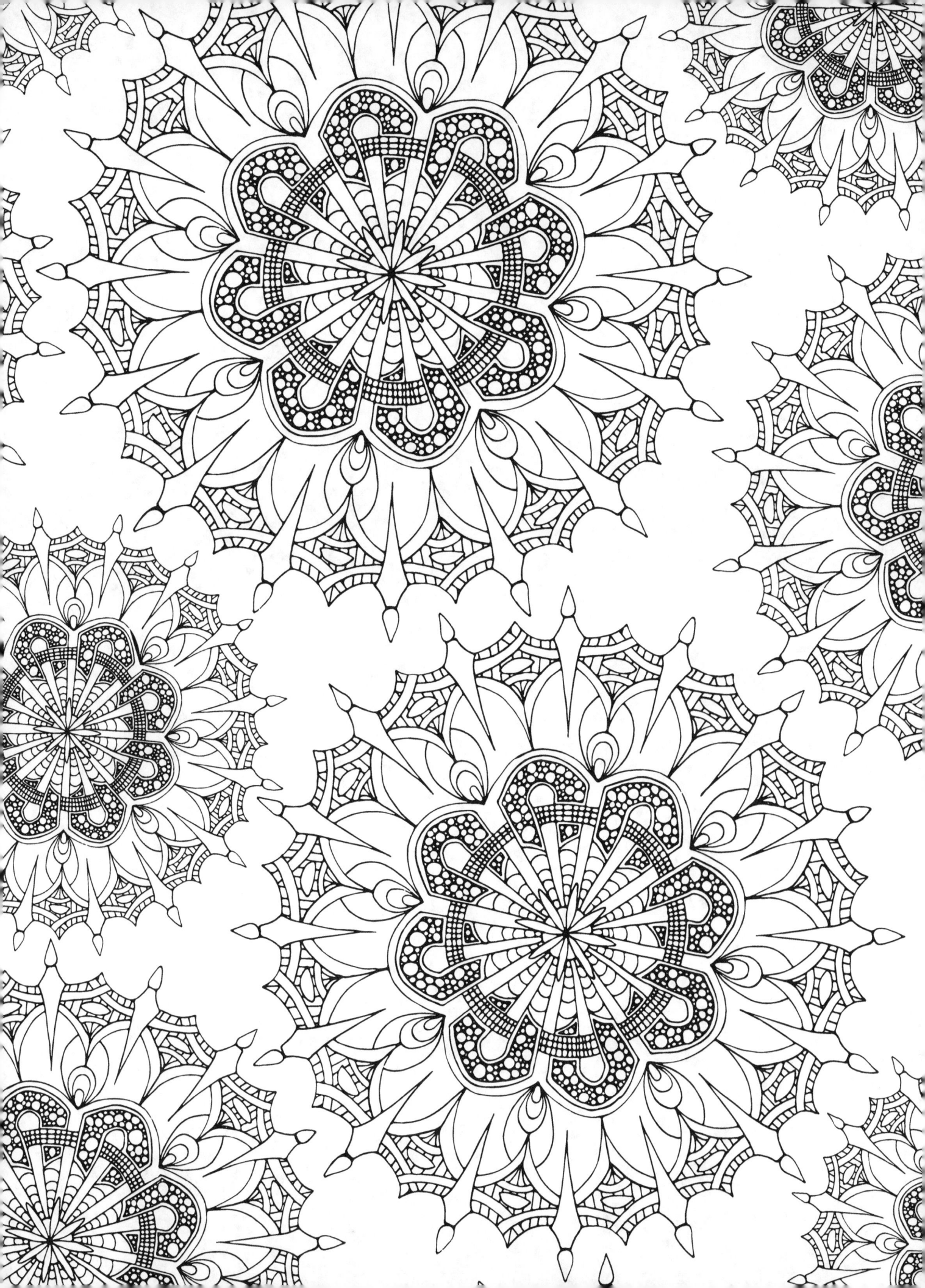

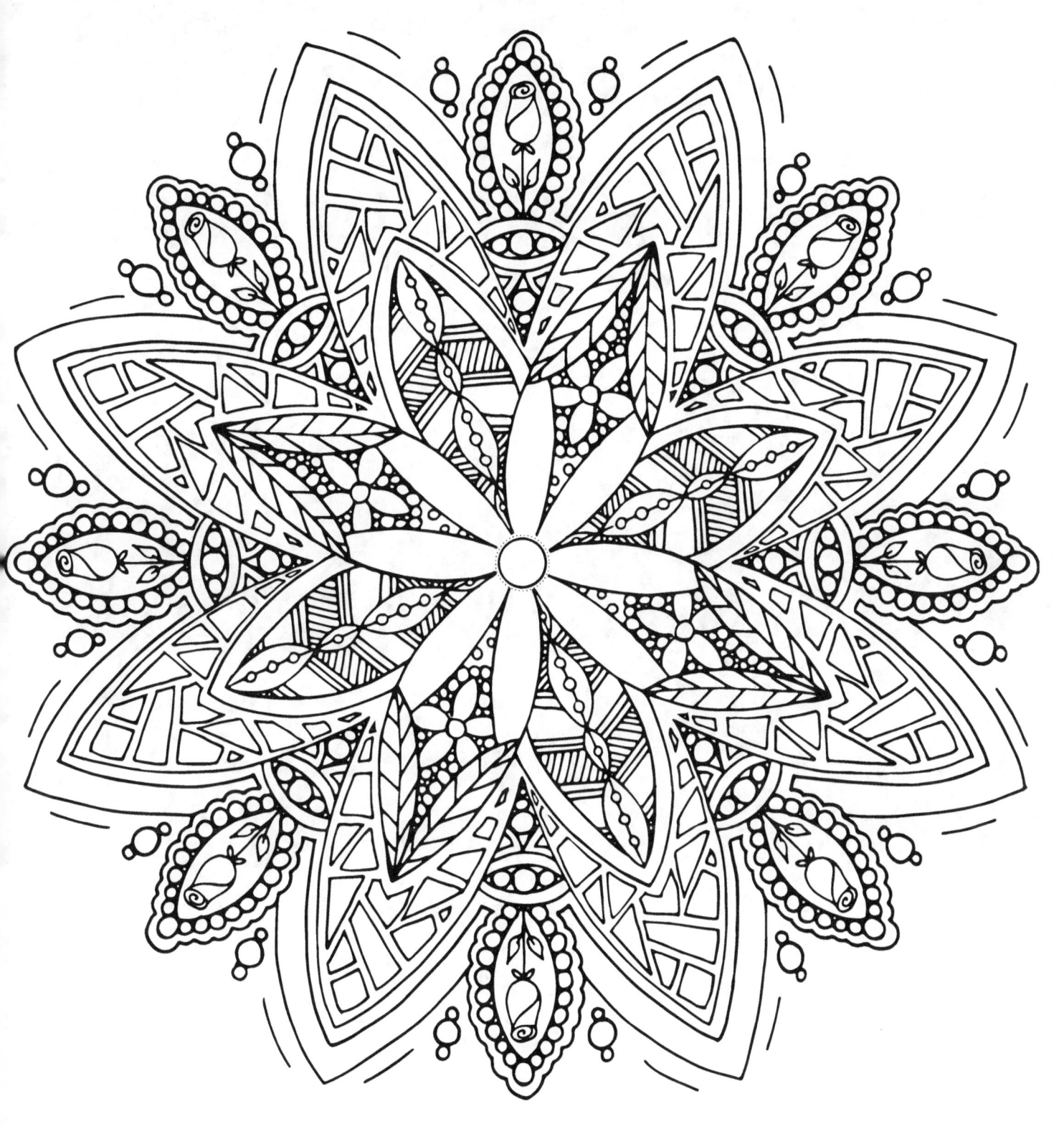

BE YOURSELF, BECAUSE AN ORIGINAL IS WORTH MORE THAN A COPY.

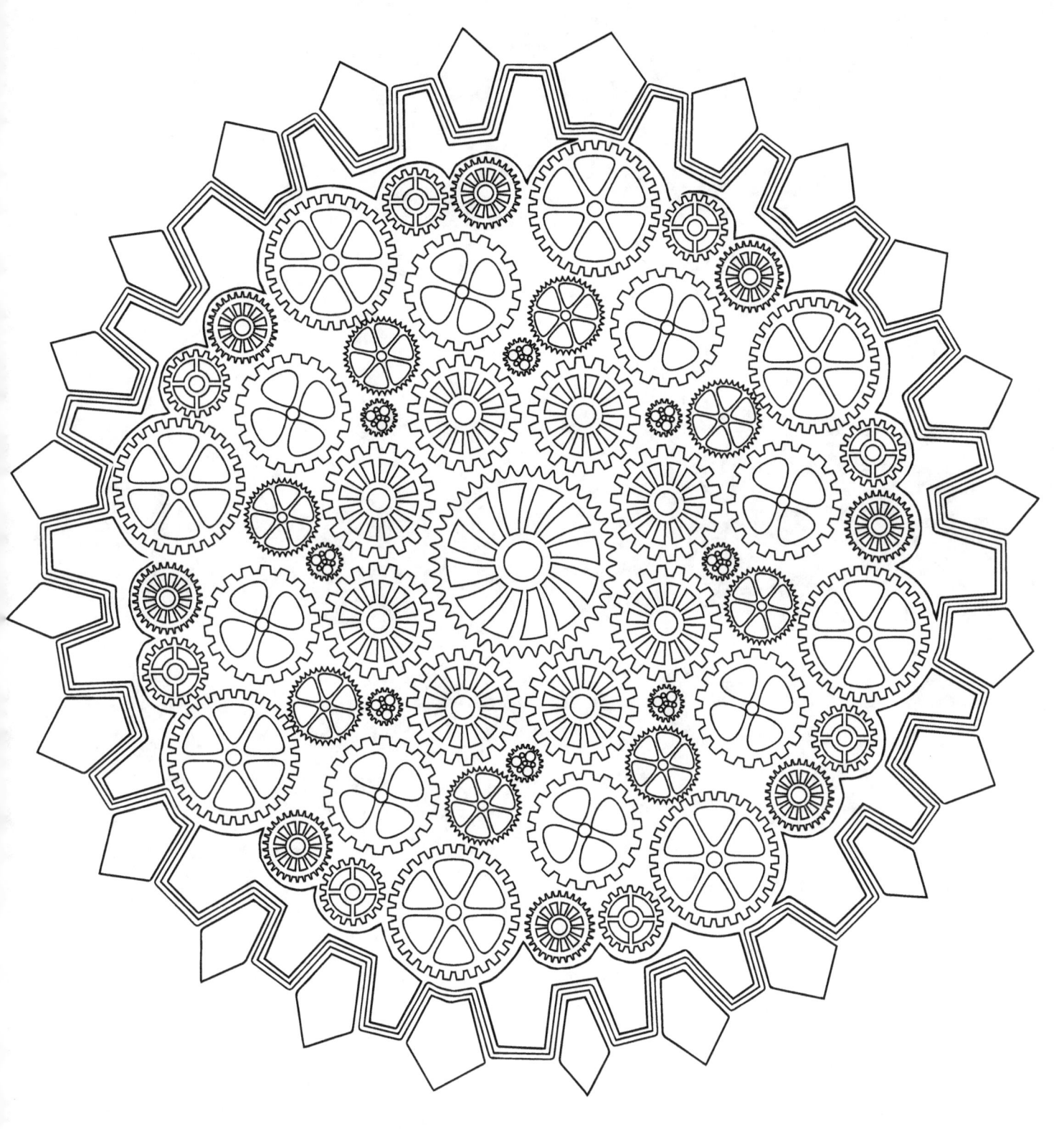

LIFE IS LIKE A TEN SPEED BIKE.
MOST OF US HAVE GEARS WE NEVER USE.

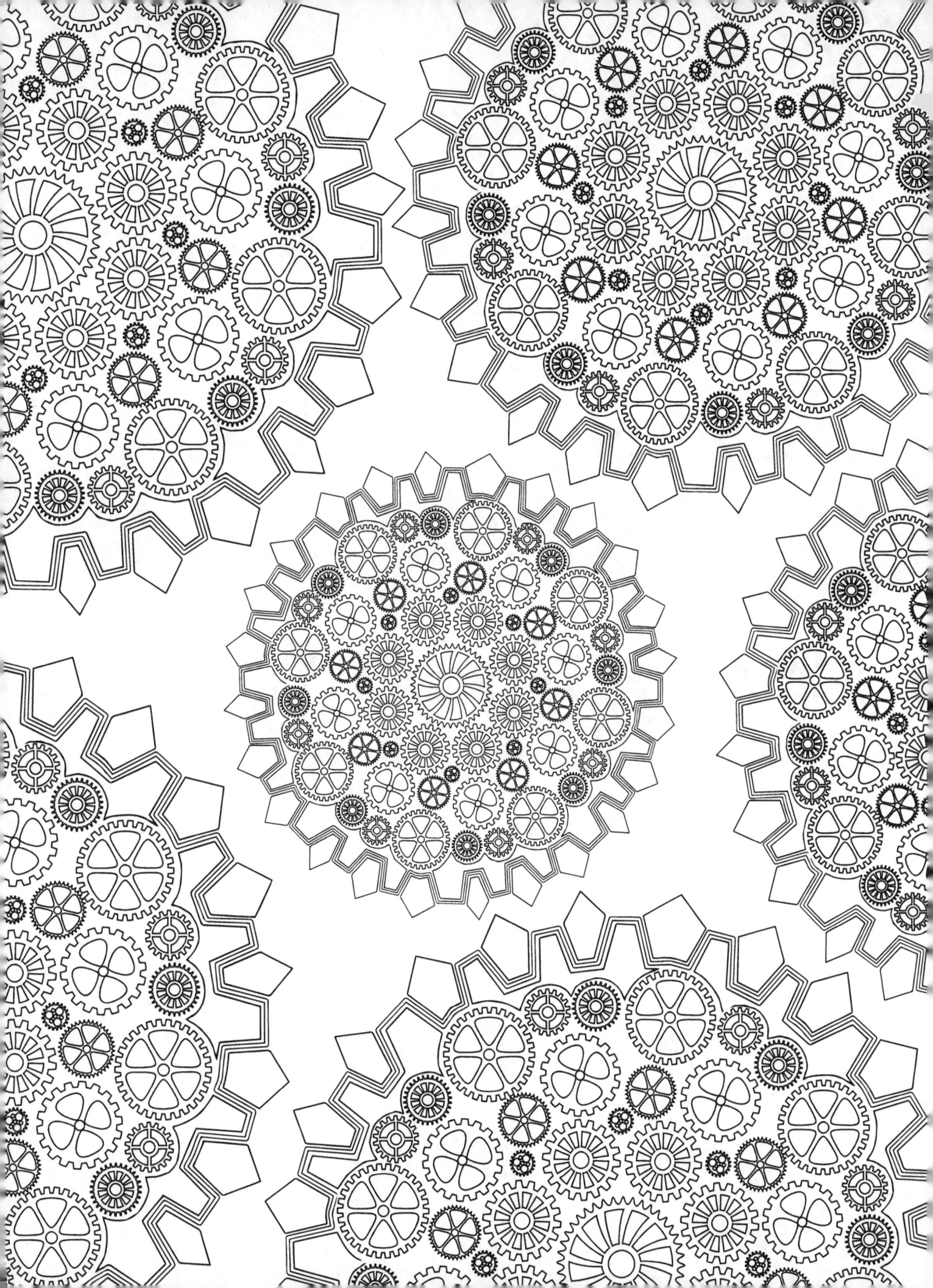

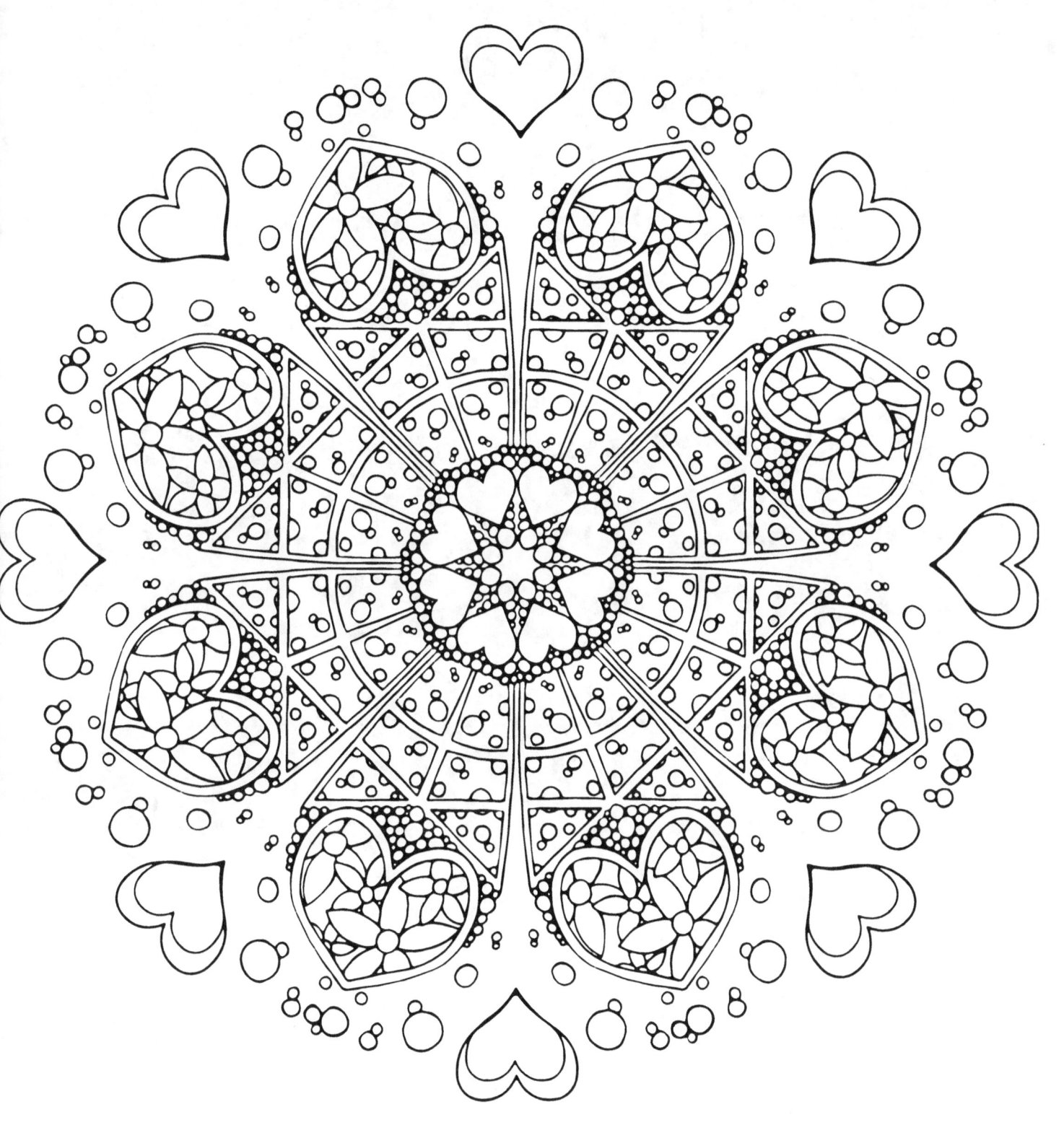

LOVE YOU FOR ALL THAT YOU ARE,
ALL THAT YOU HAVE BEEN,
AND ALL YOU ARE YET TO BE.

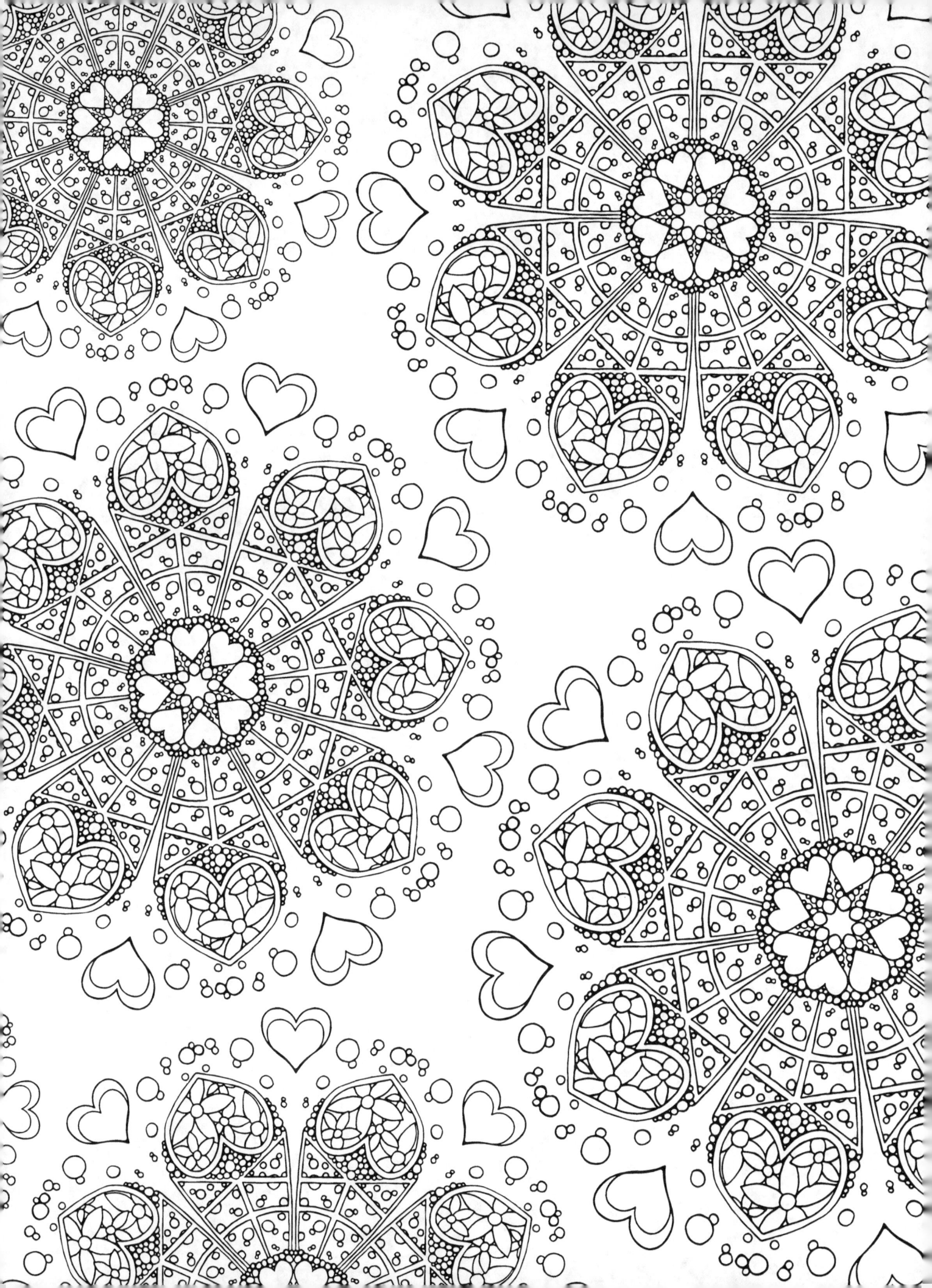

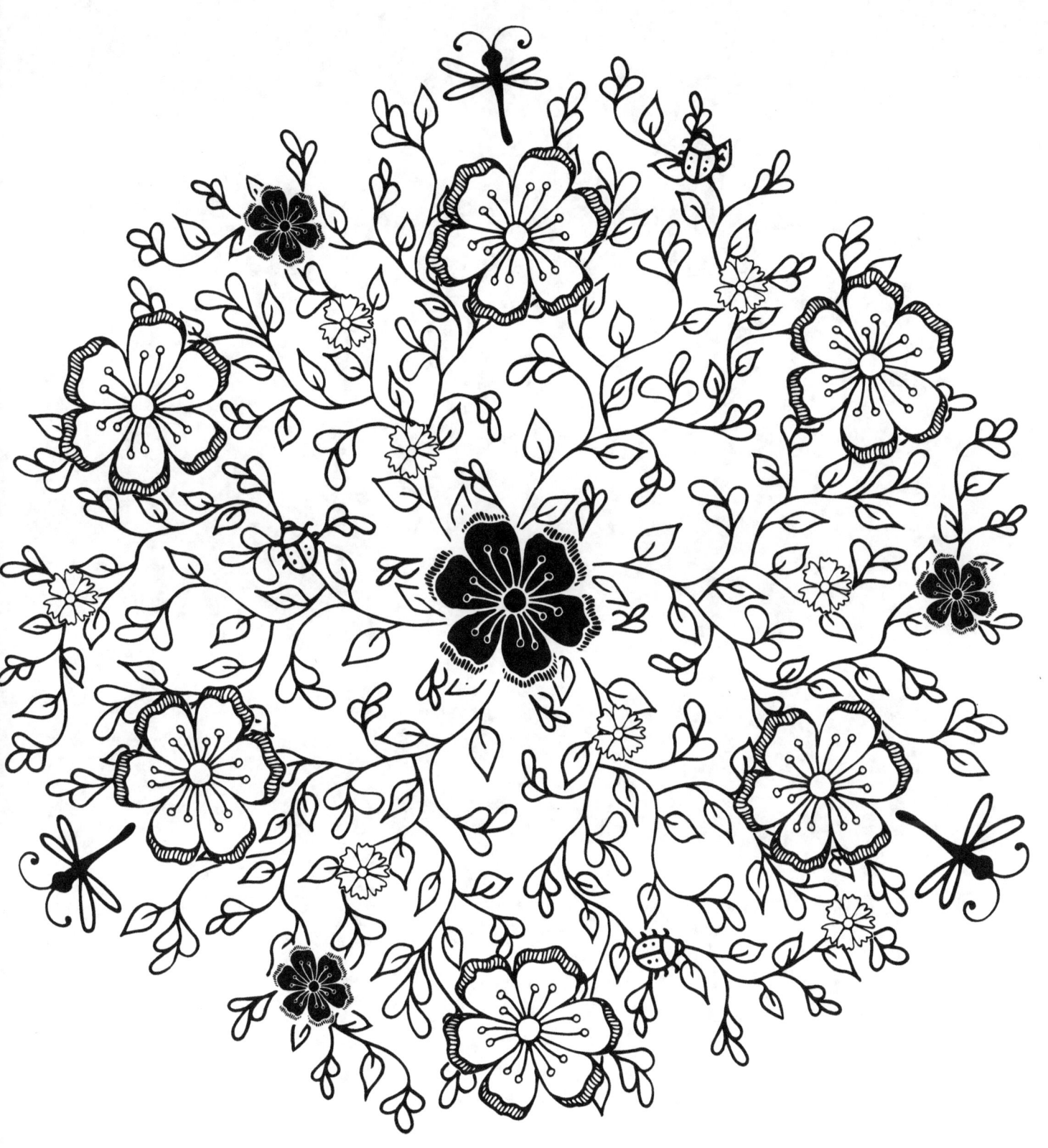

A LIFE WITHOUT DREAMS IS LIKE A GARDEN
WITHOUT FLOWERS.

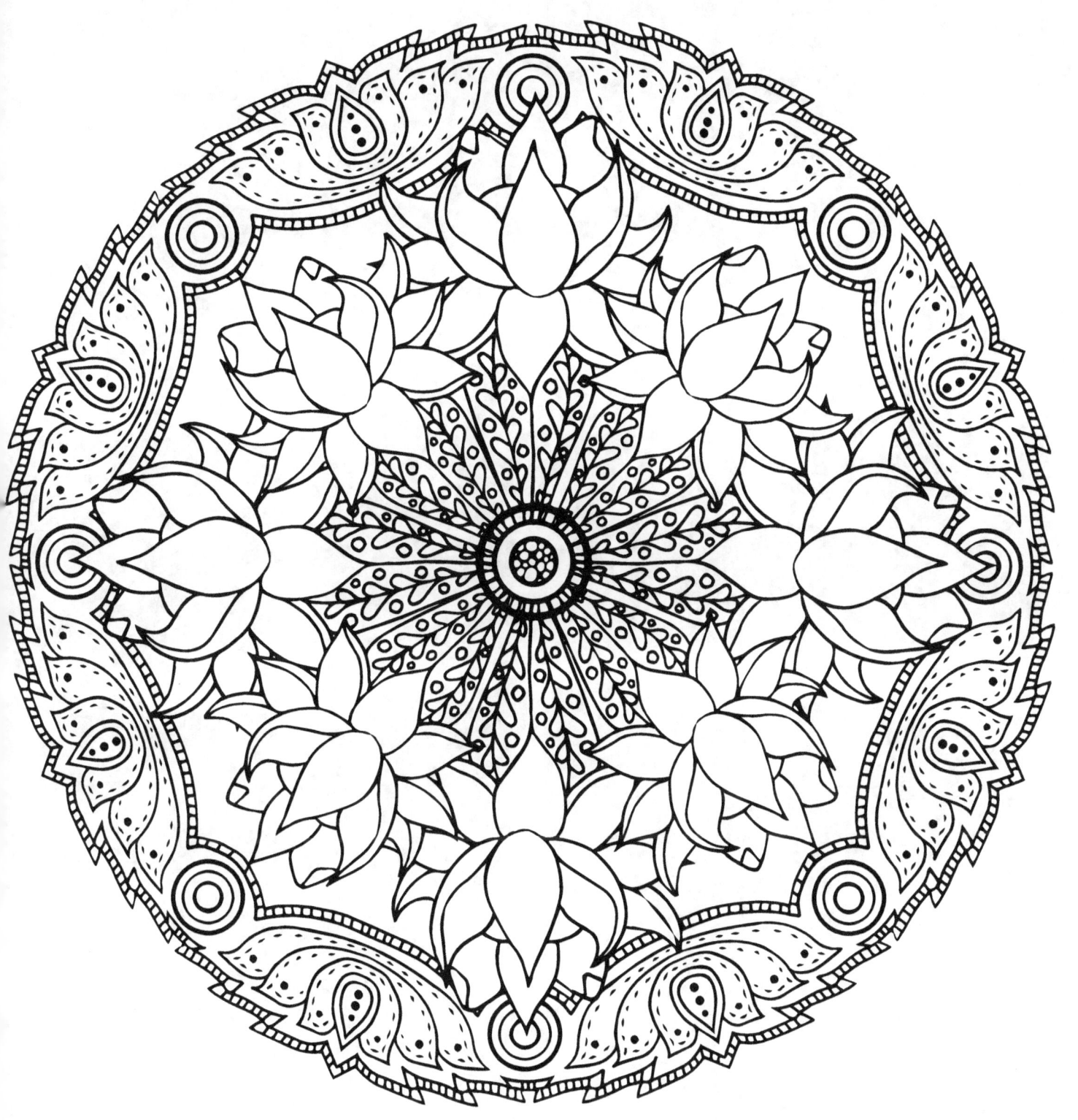

Out of the mud of your fears, pain & confusion: the lotus flower of your inner heart will spontaneously grow.

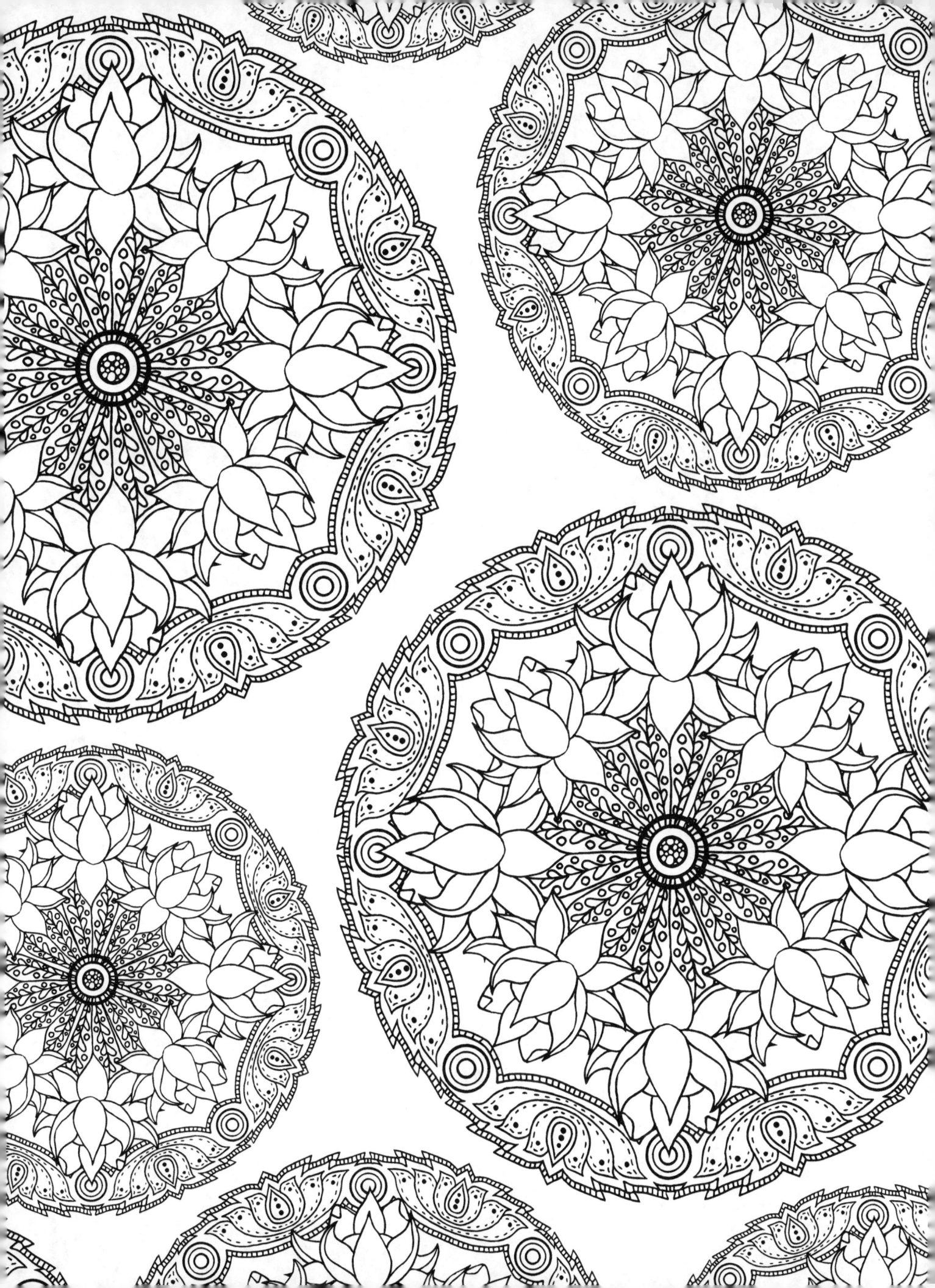

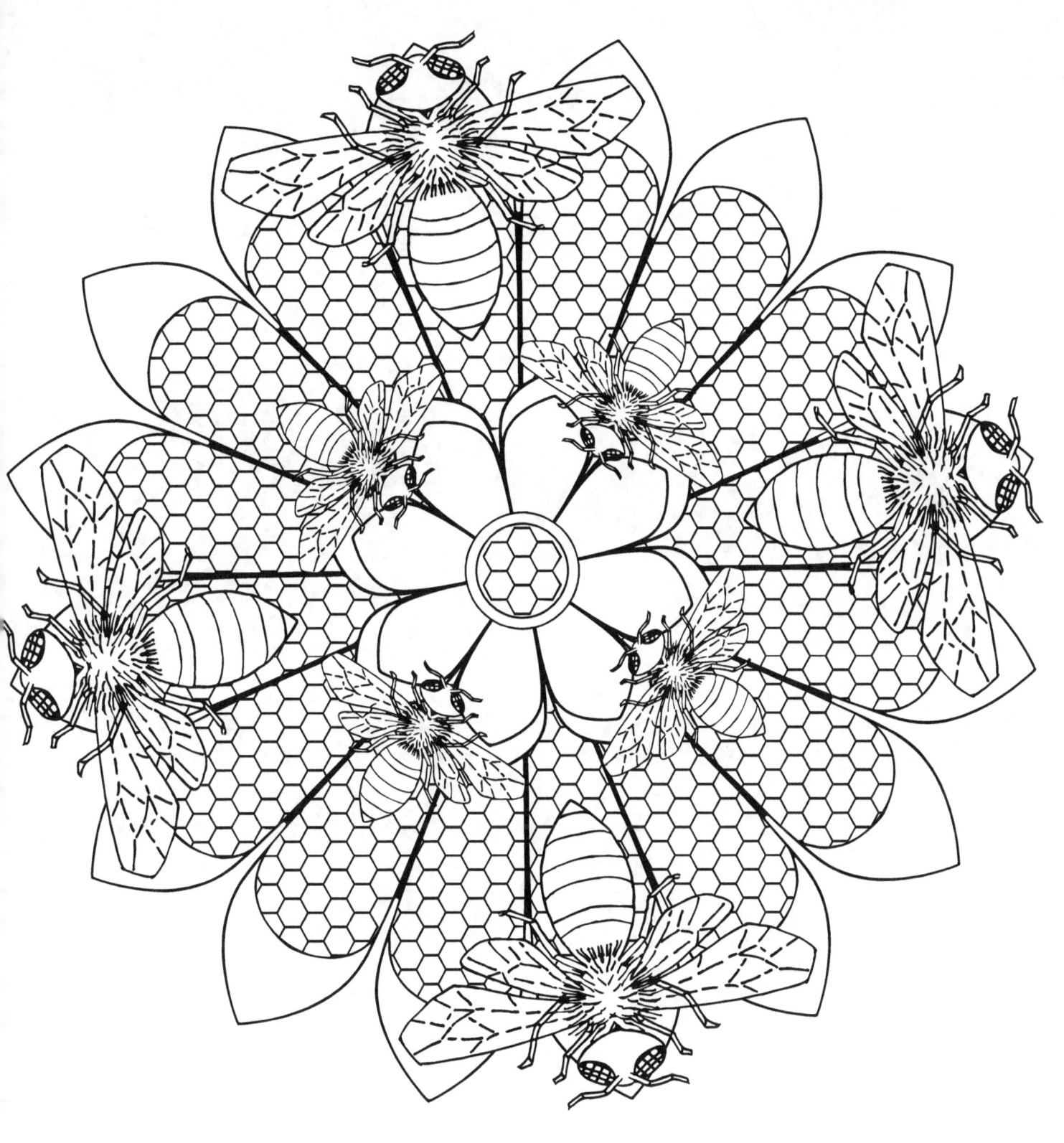

HOPE IS THE ONLY BEE THAT MAKES HONEY
WITHOUT FLOWERS.

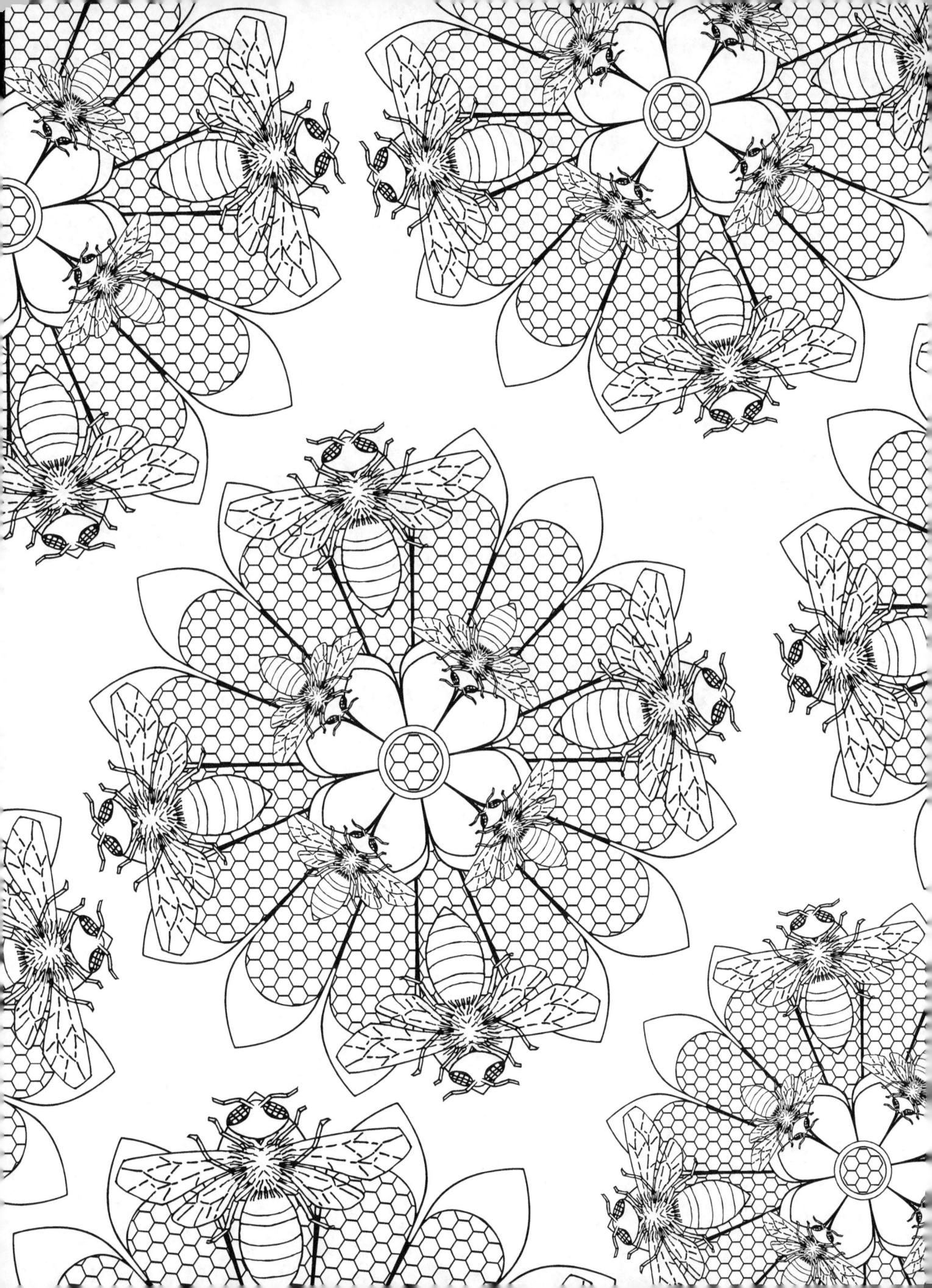

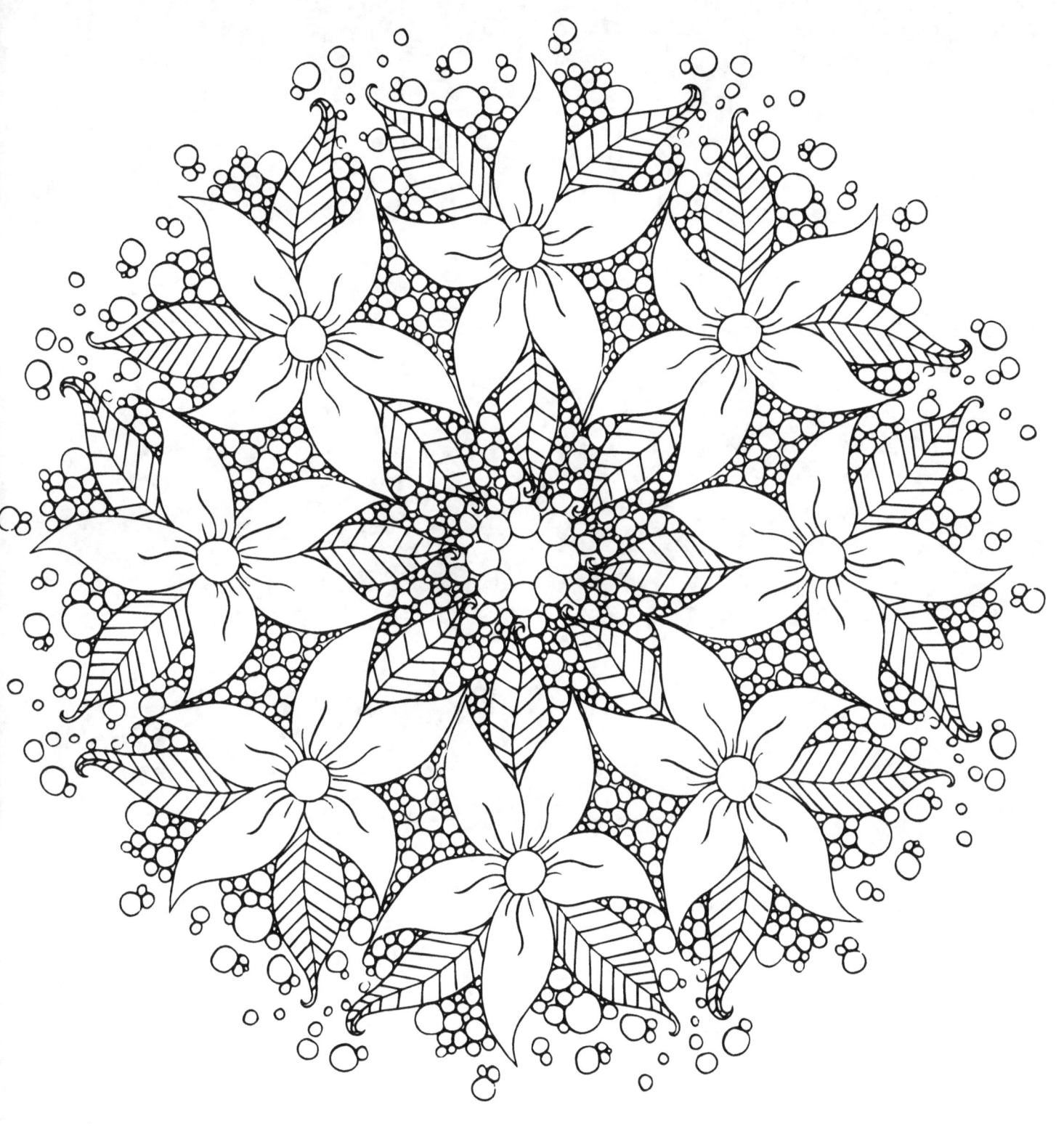

A FLOWER CANNOT BLOSSOM WITHOUT SUNSHINE AND MAN CANNOT LIVE WITHOUT LOVE.

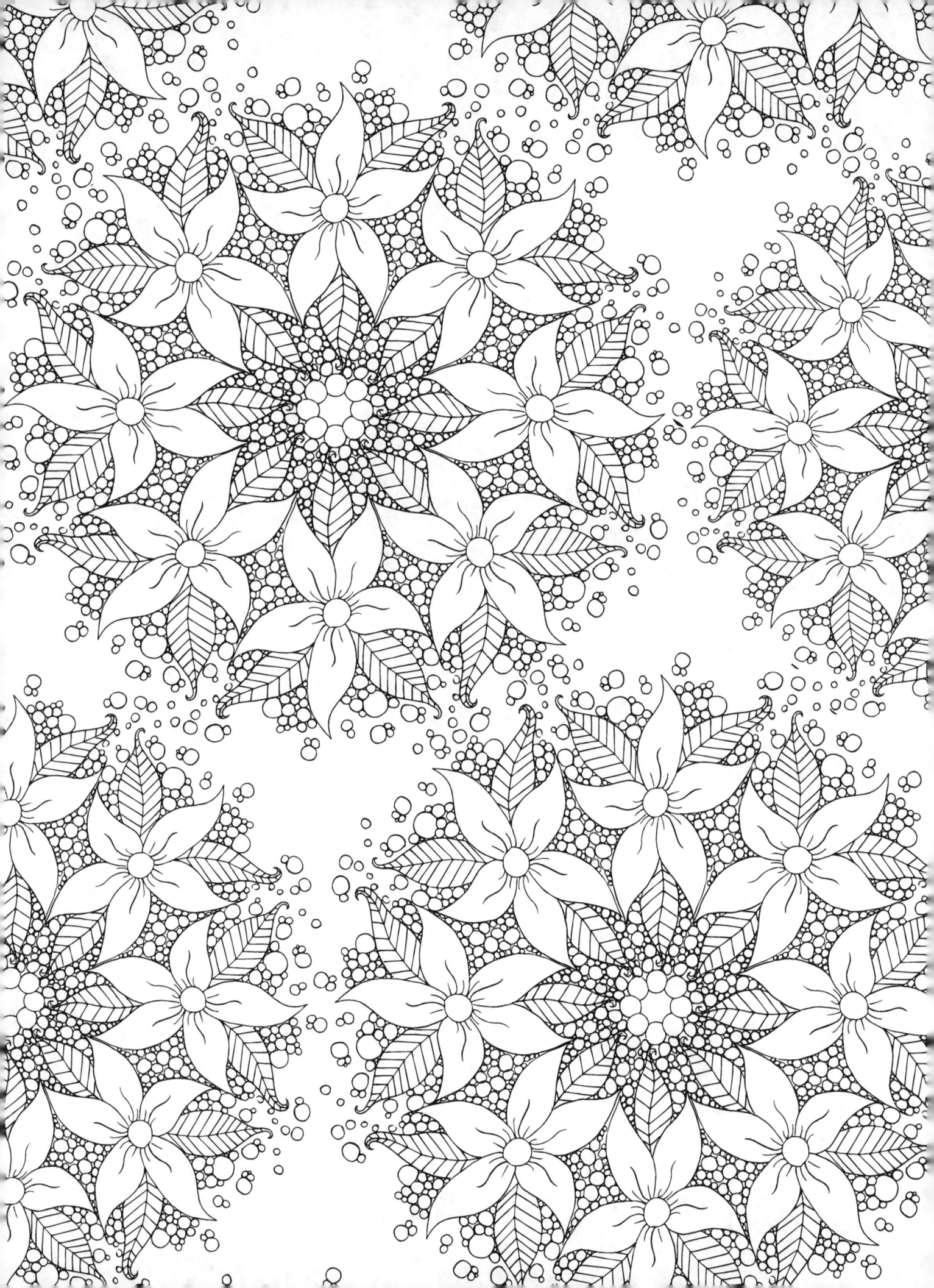

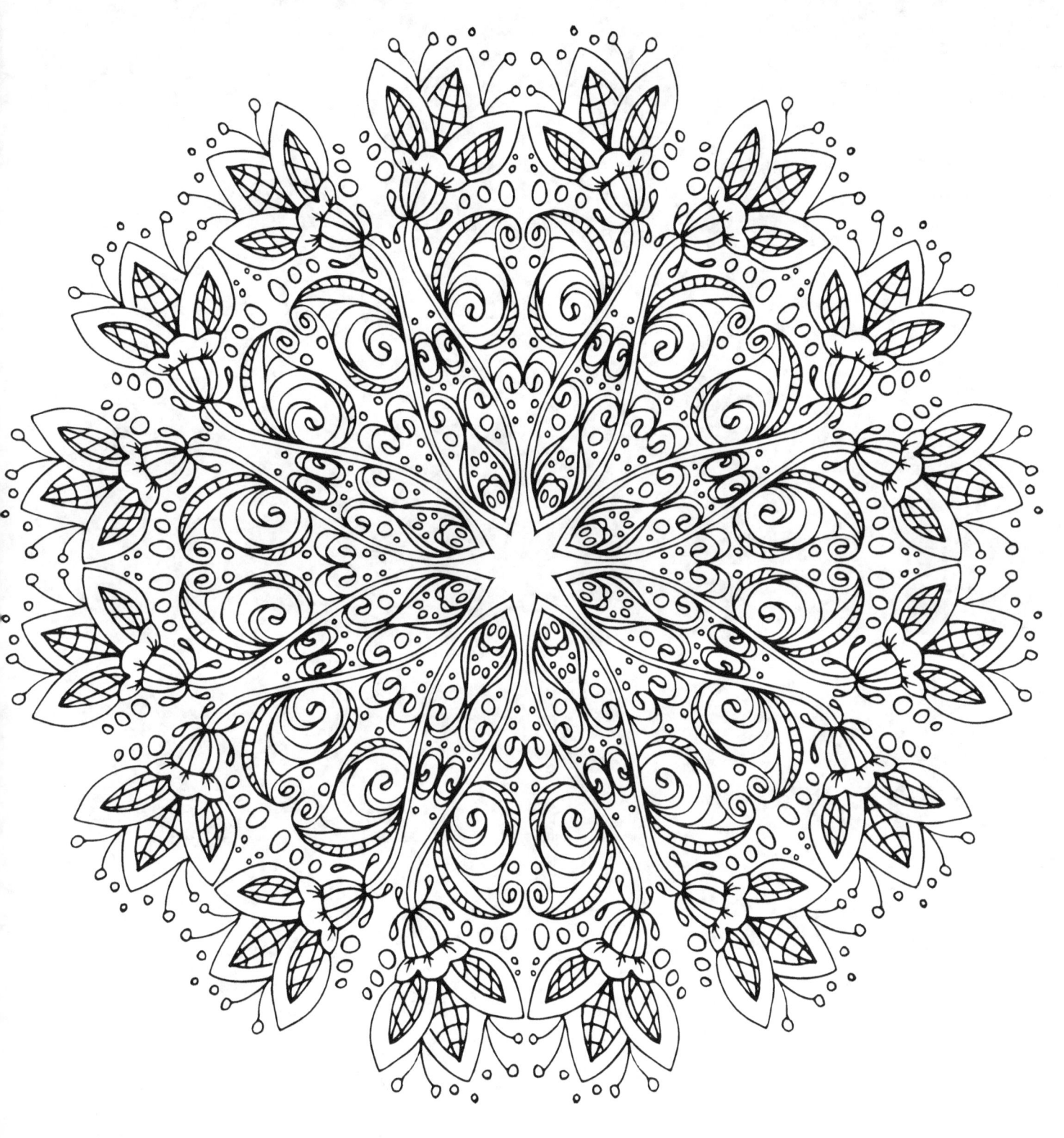

THE GREATEST PLEASURE IN LIFE IS DOING WHAT PEOPLE SAY YOU CANNOT DO.

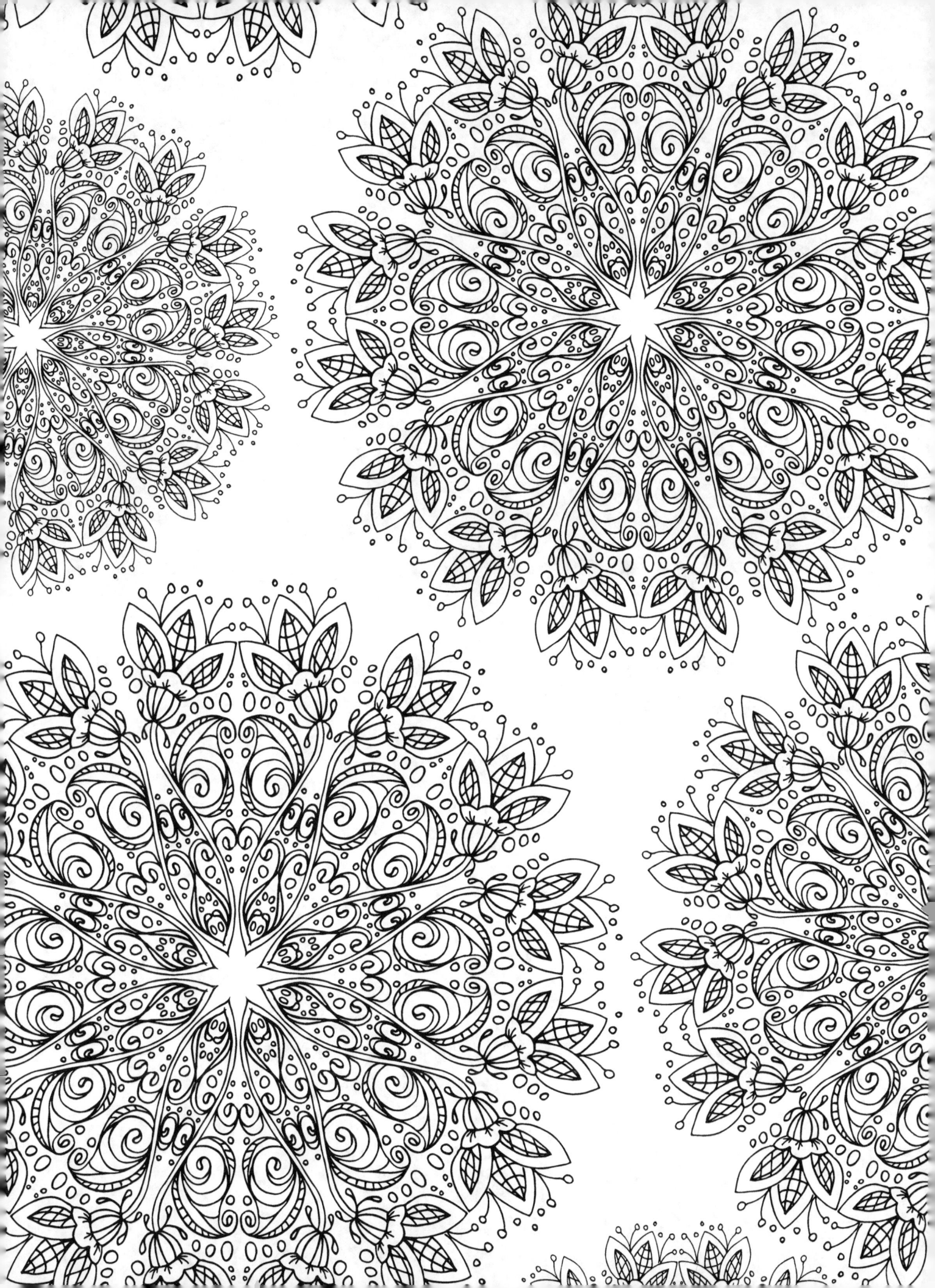

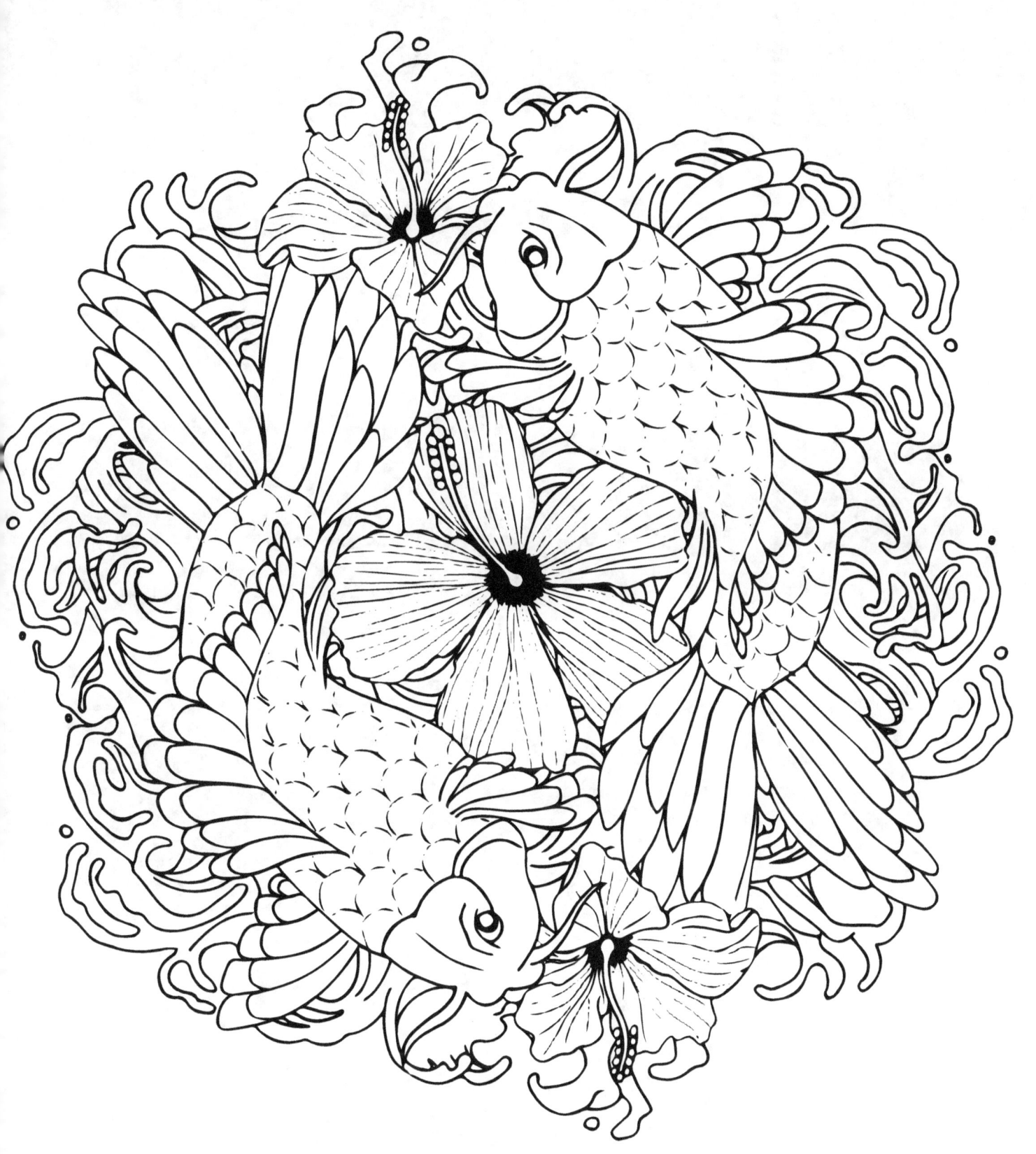

GREAT WORKS ARE PERFORMED NOT BY STRENGTH, BUT BY PERSEVERANCE.

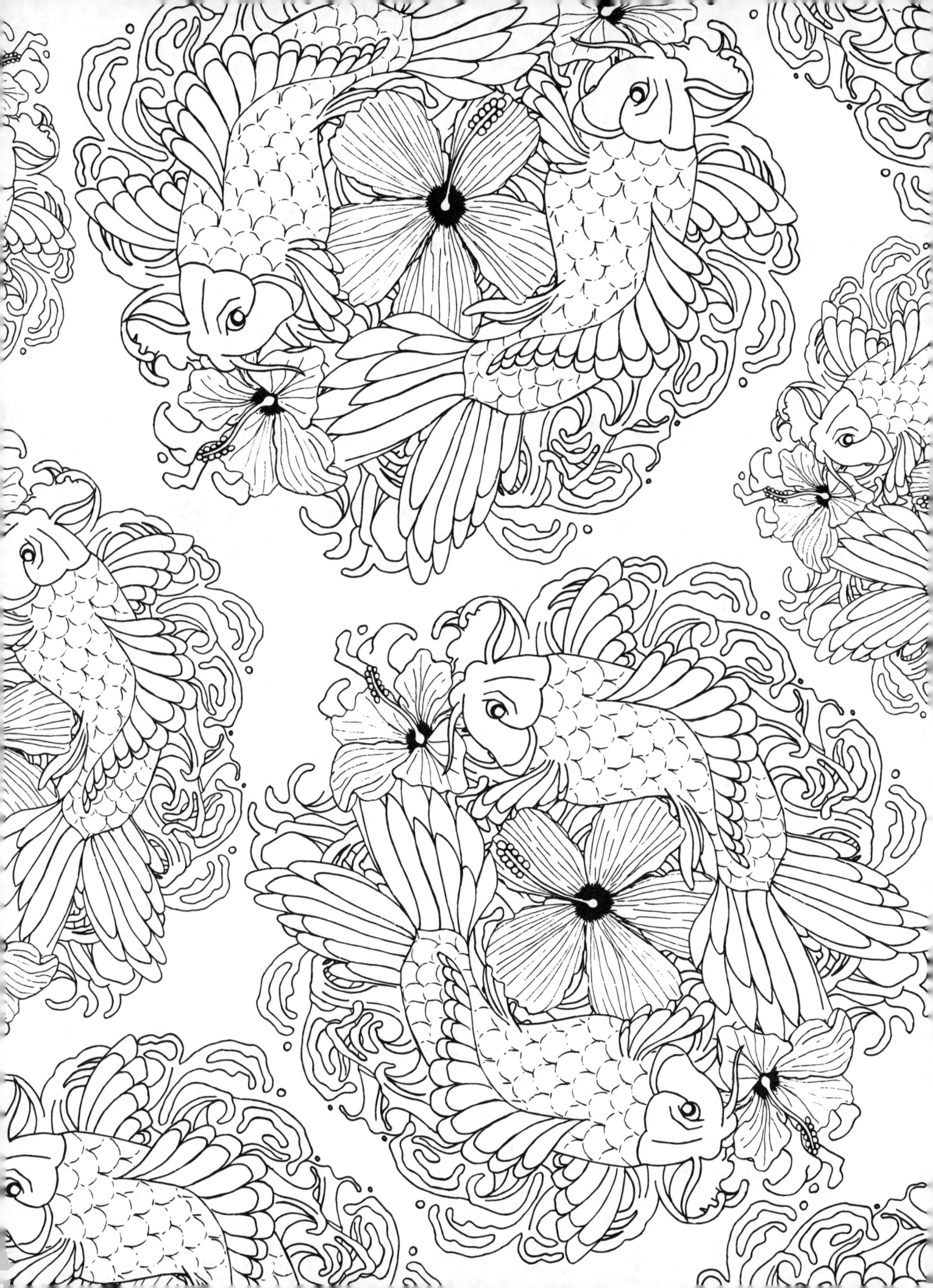

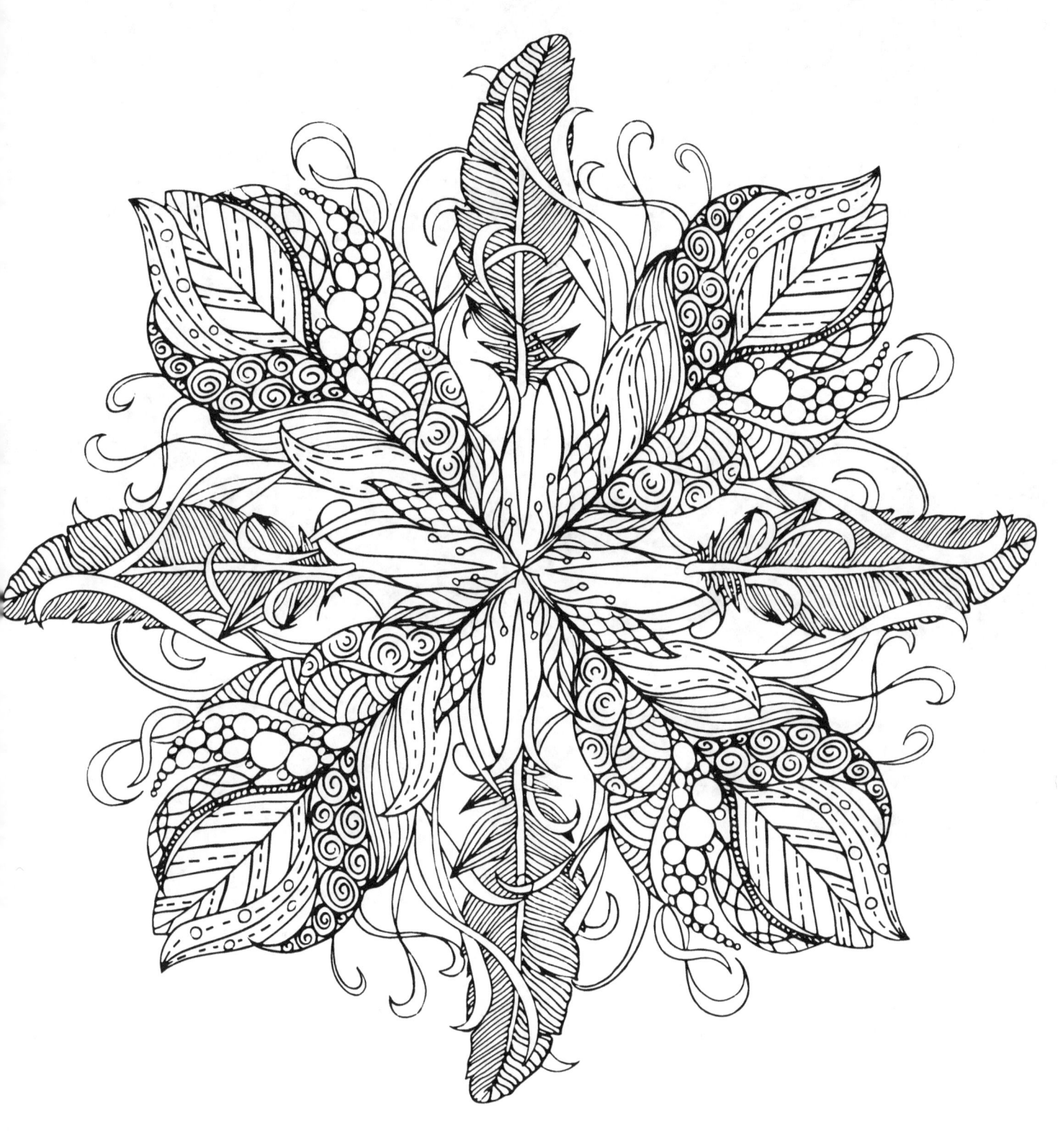

CHALLENGES MAKE LIFE INTERESTING.
OVERCOMING THEM MAKES LIFE MEANINGFUL.

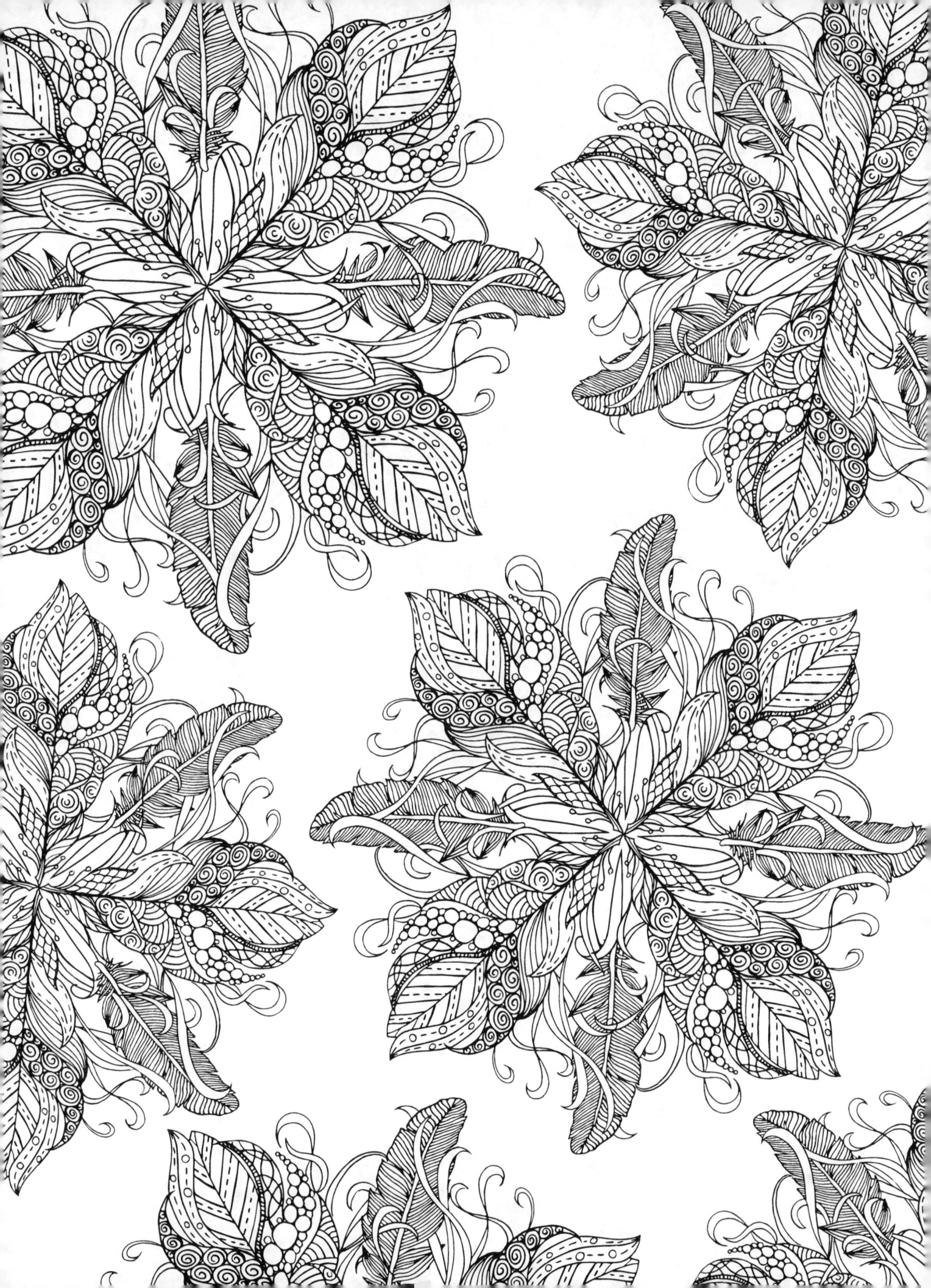

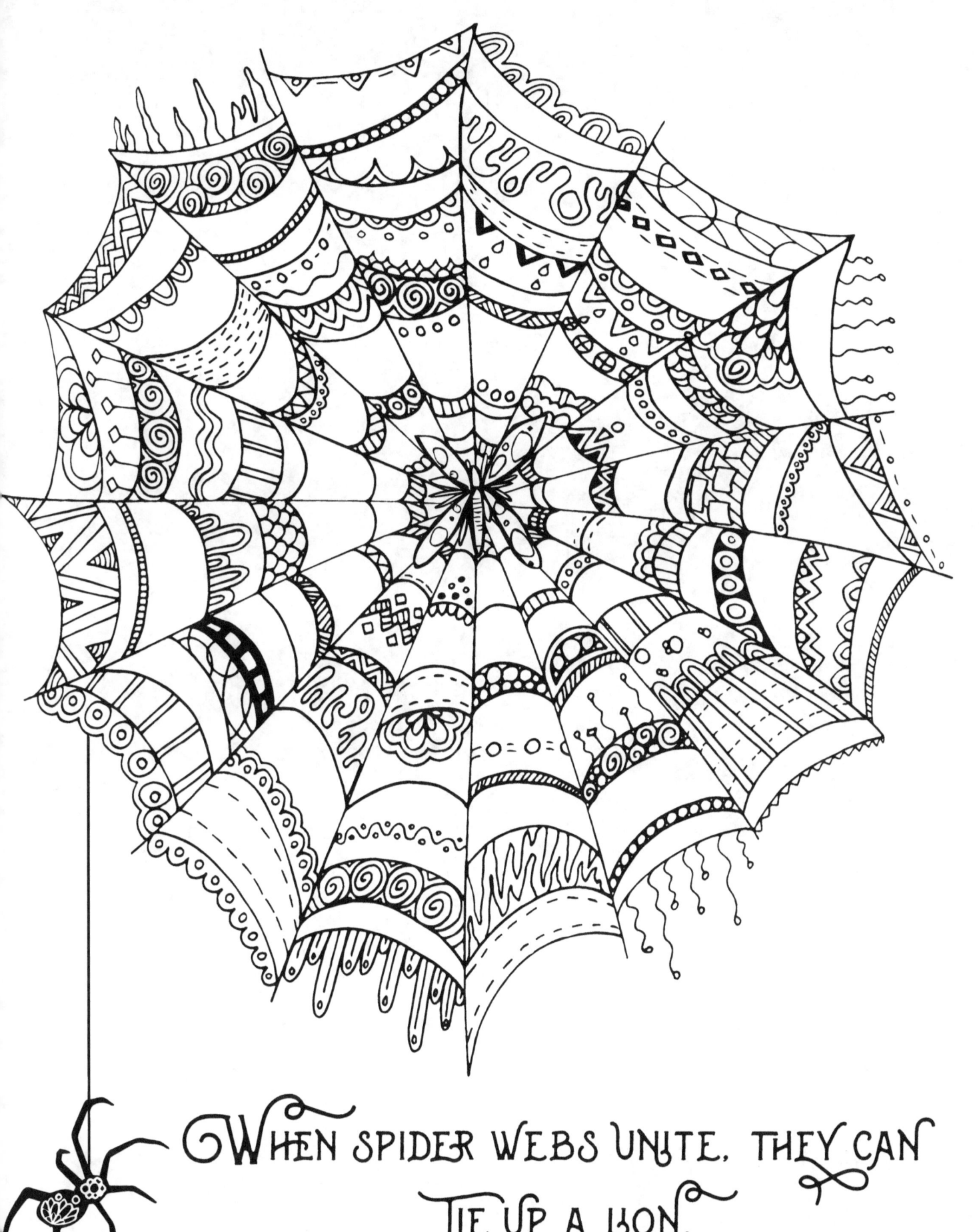

WHEN SPIDER WEBS UNITE, THEY CAN TIE UP A LION.

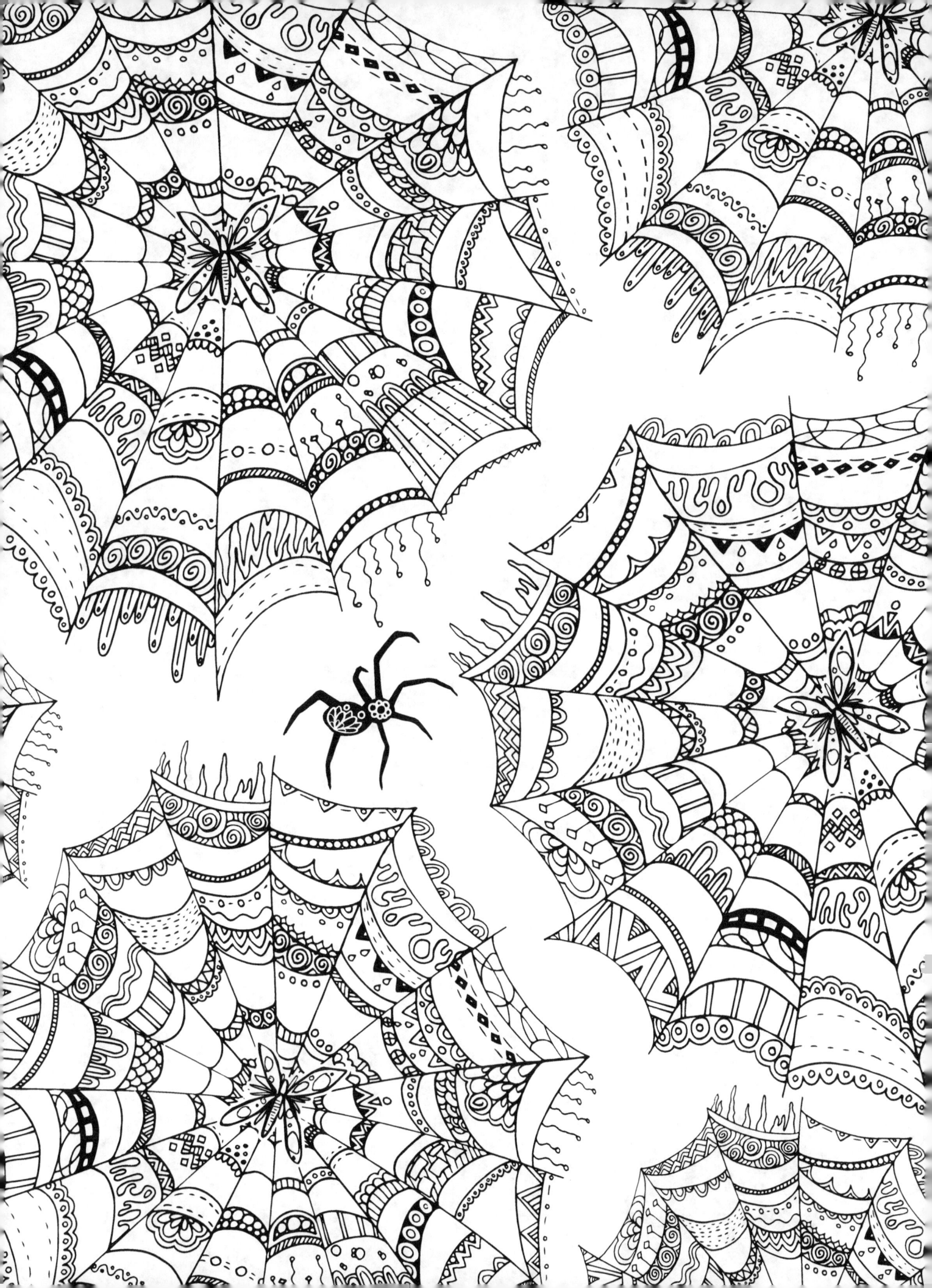

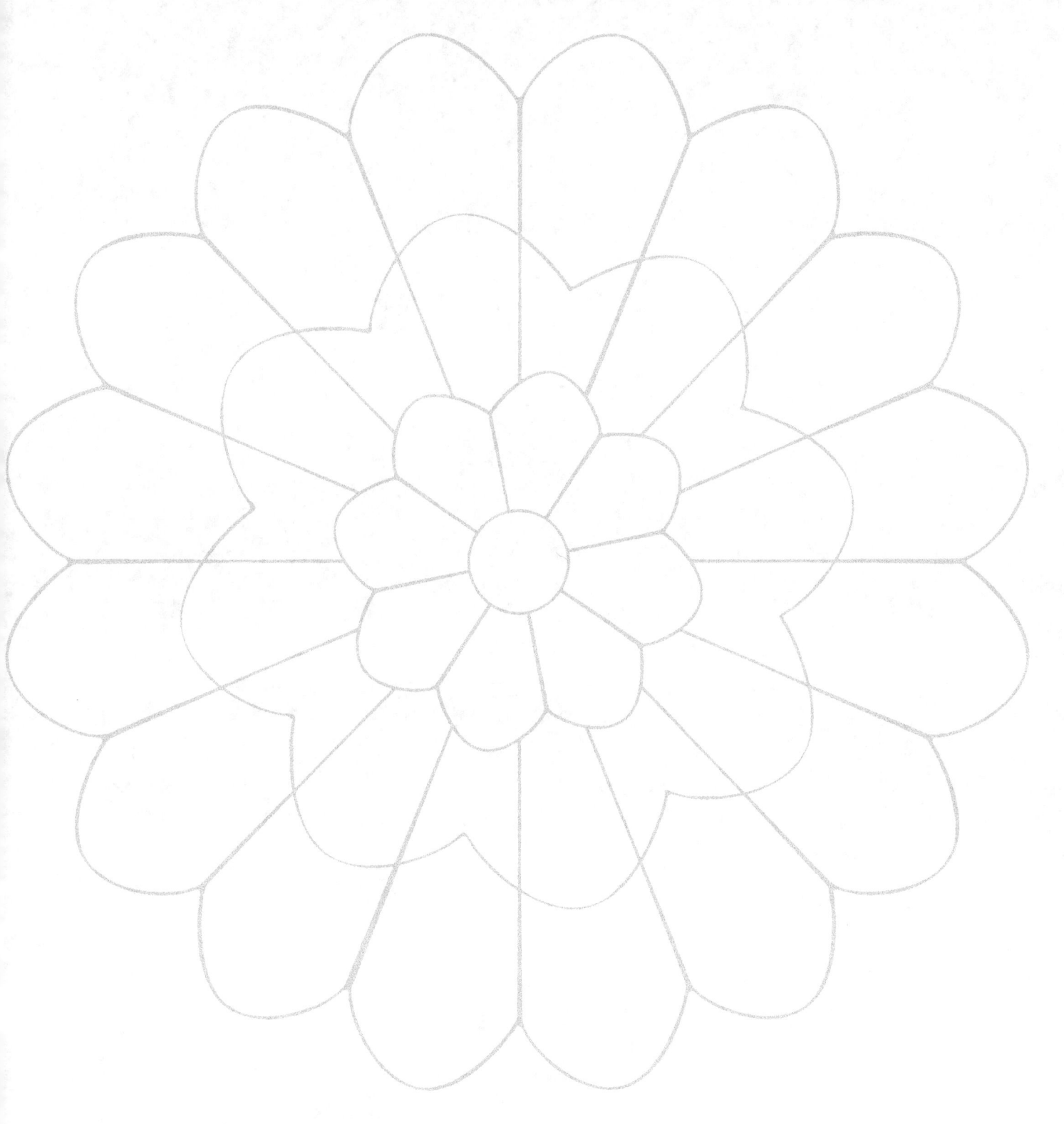

IF IT DOESN'T CHALLENGE YOU IT WON'T CHANGE YOU.

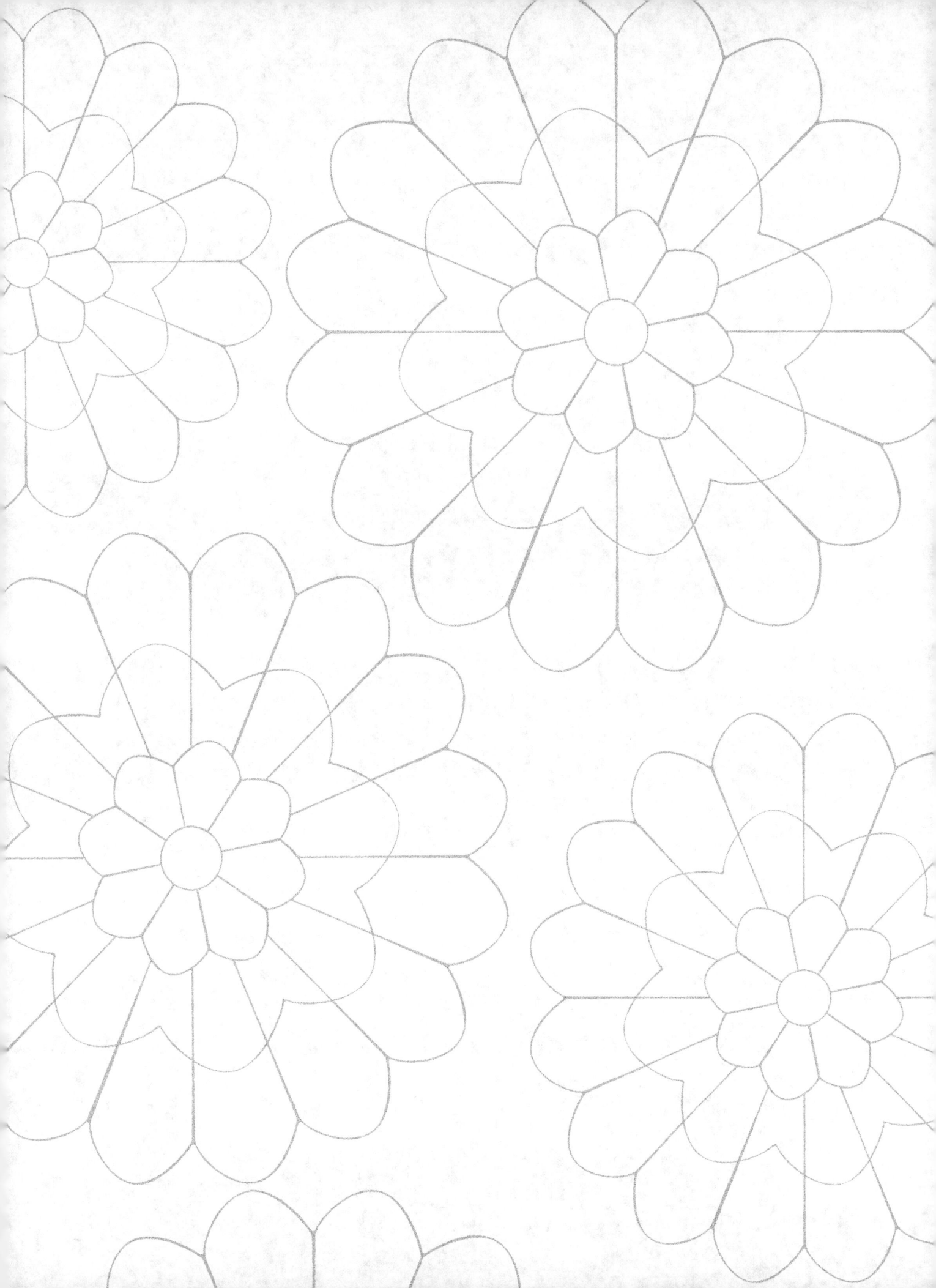

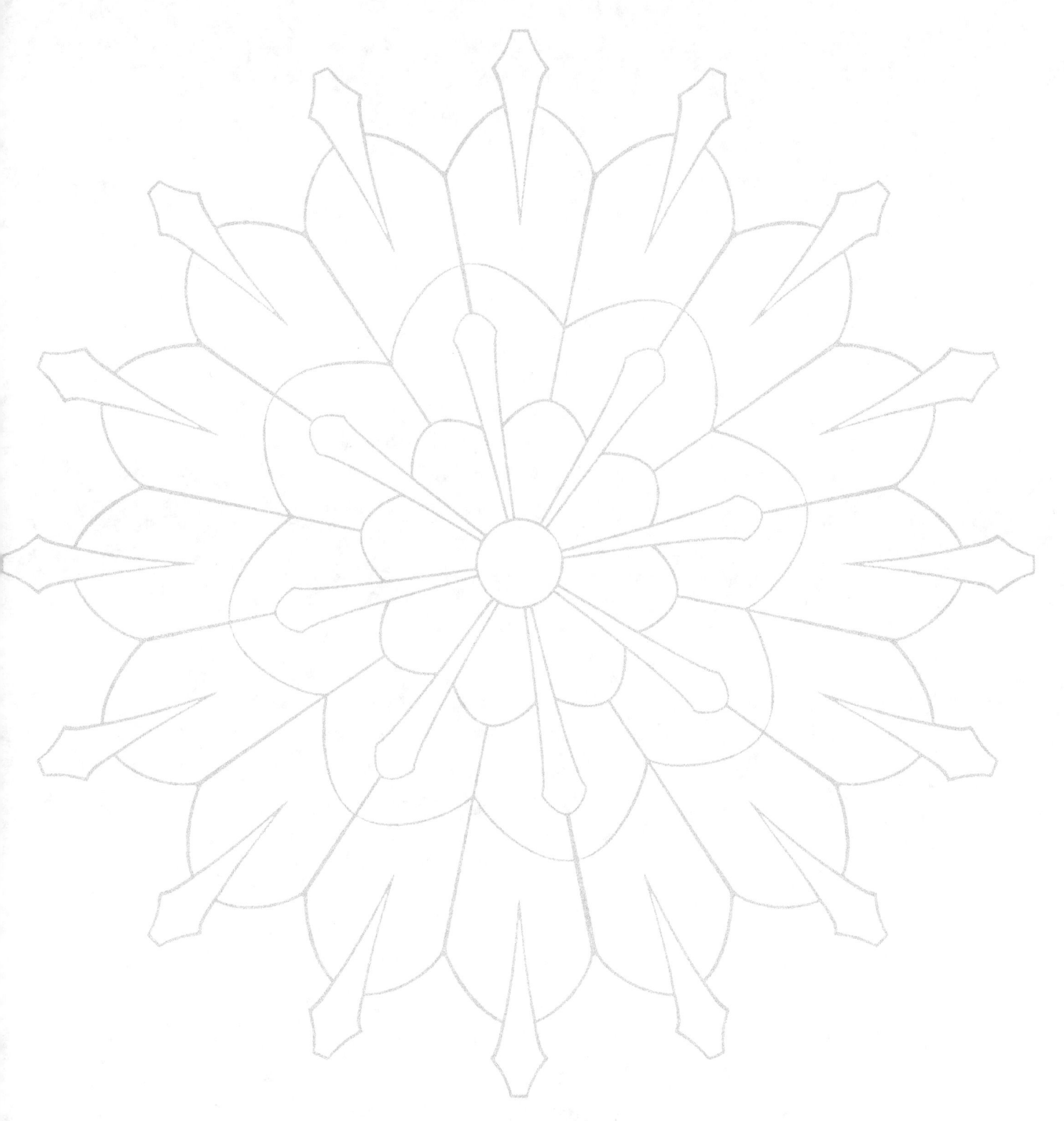

THE ONLY PERSON YOU SHOULD TRY TO BE
BETTER THAN IS THE PERSON
YOU WERE YESTERDAY.

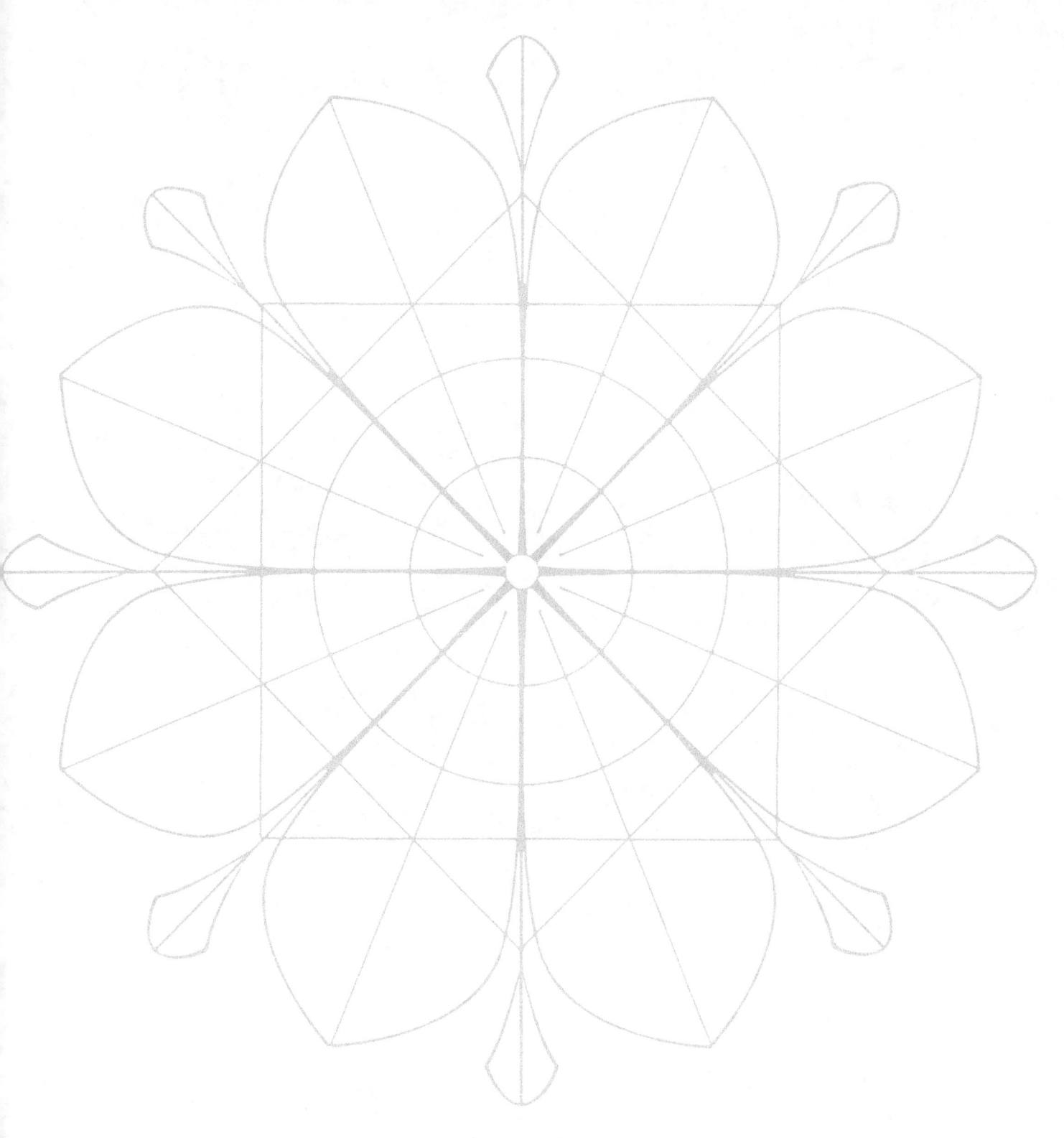

YOUR HEART IS JUST THE BEATBOX FOR THE
SONG OF YOUR LIFE.

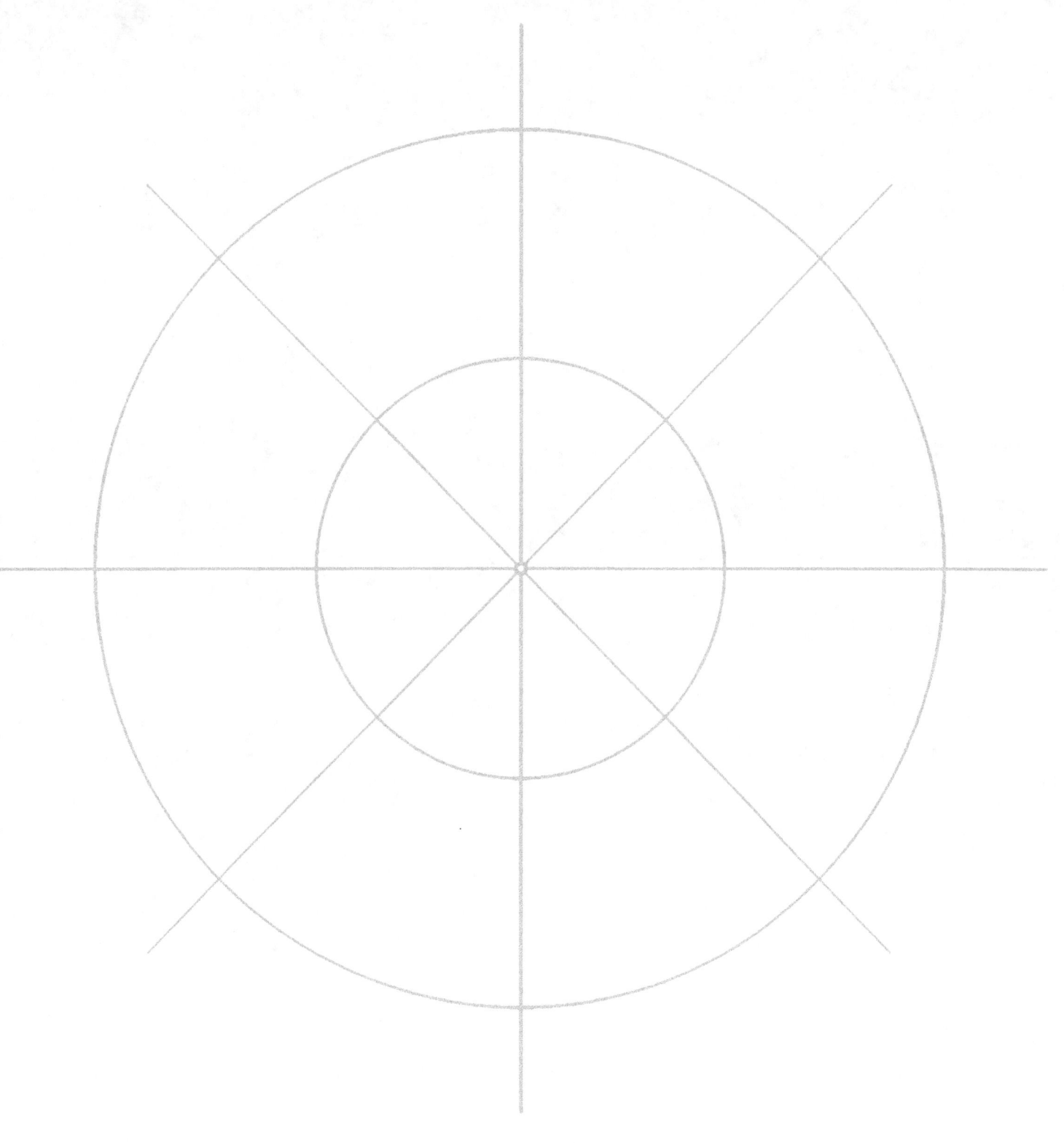

SOMEDAYS YOU JUST HAVE TO CREATE YOUR OWN SUNSHINE.

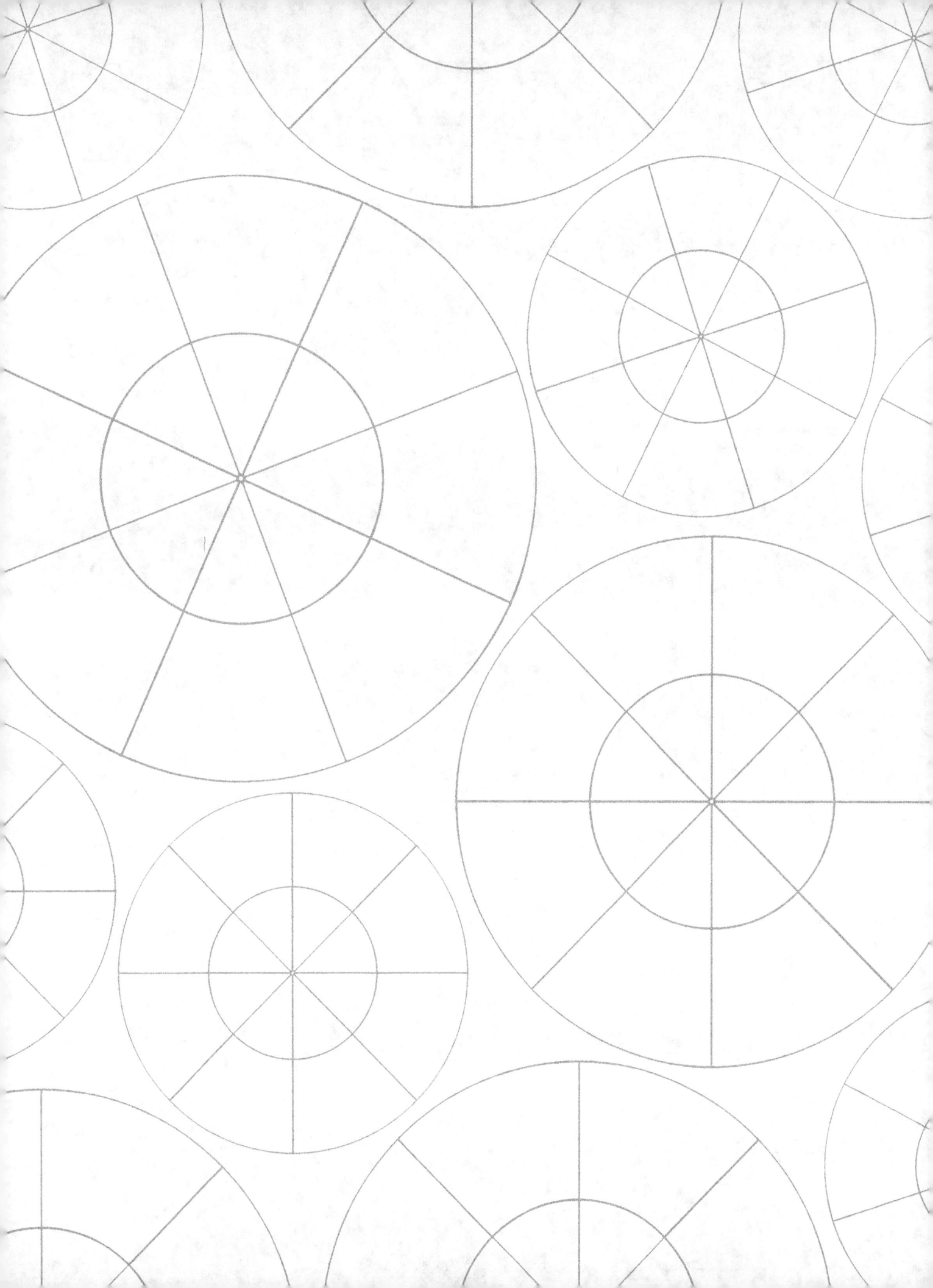

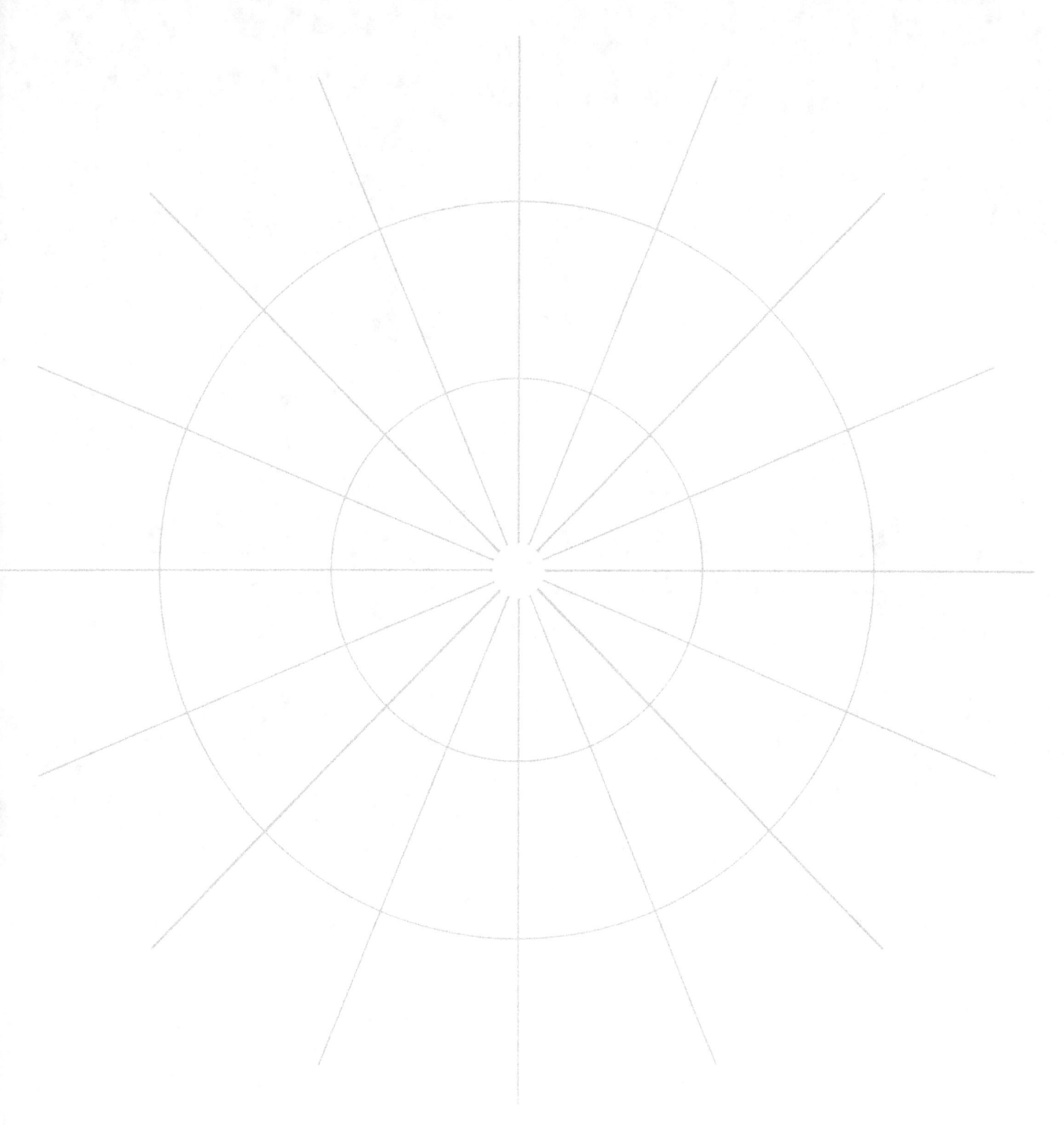

LAUGHTER IS TIMELESS, IMAGINATION HAS NO AGE, AND DREAMS ARE FOREVER.

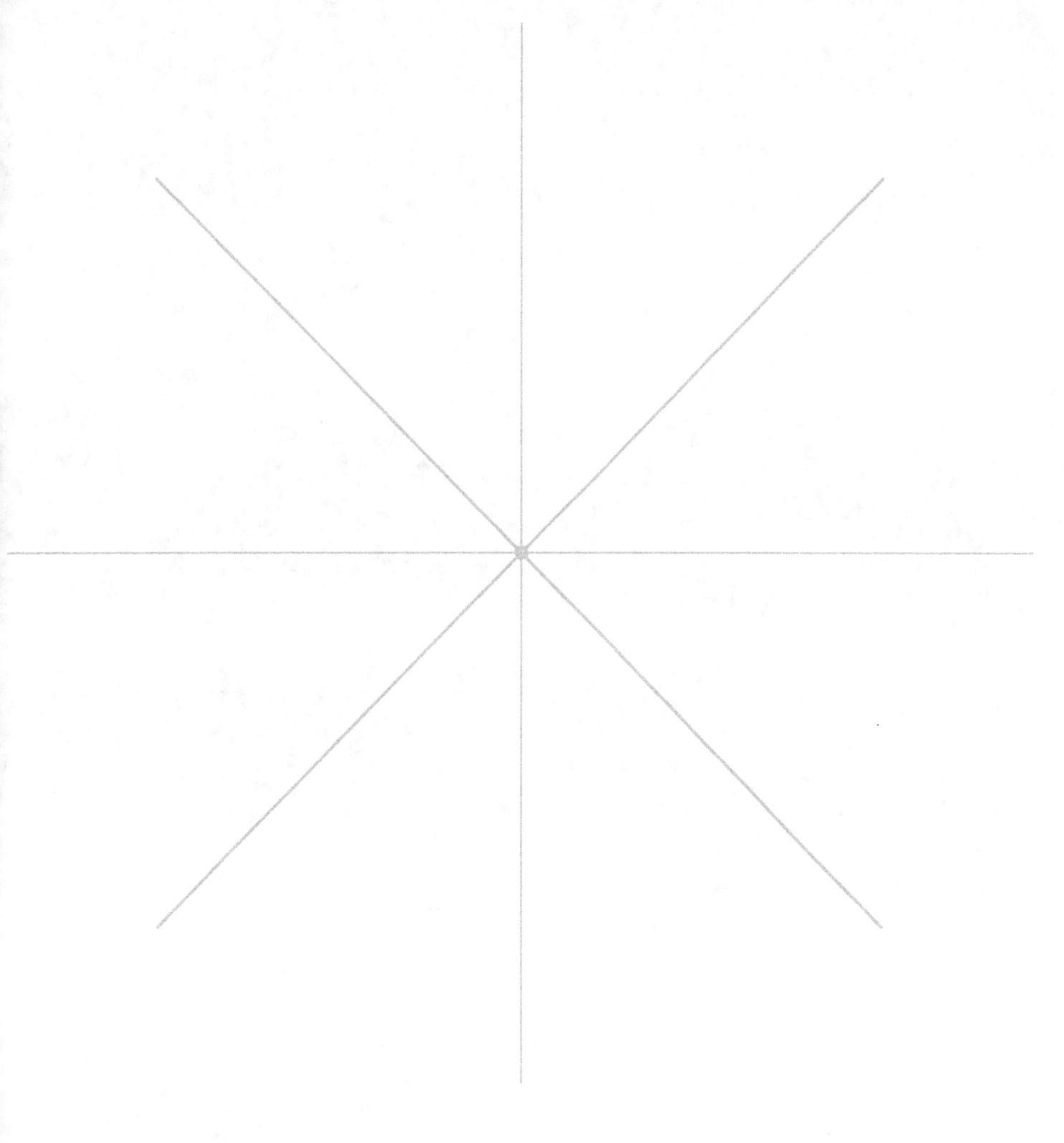

BE SOMEBODY WHO MAKES EVERYBODY FEEL
LIKE A SOMEBODY.